ERRATA

EX FAMILIA

*Grandparents, Parents,
and Children
Adjust to Divorce*

Colleen Leahy Johnson

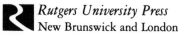

Rutgers University Press
New Brunswick and London

Library of Congress Cataloging-in-Publication Data

Johnson, Colleen Leahy, 1932–
    Ex familia : grandparents, parents, and children adjust to
divorce / Colleen Leahy Johnson.
        p.   cm.
    Bibliography: p.
    Includes index.
    ISBN 0-8135-1325-1   ISBN 0-8135-1326-X (pbk.)
    1. Divorced parents—California—Family relationships—
Case studies.   2. Grandparent and child—California—Case
studies.   3. Intergenerational relations—California—Case
studies.   I. Title.
HQ835.C2J65   1988
306.8'9—dc19   88-1001
                                                          CIP

British Cataloging-in-Publication information available

CONTENTS

Preface   vii

1. Introduction   1
2. The Research Approach   19
3. Cultural Directives and Intergenerational
   Relations   32
4. The Divorce   62
5. Grandparenting in Divorcing Families   87
6. Parents and Their Adult Children   116
7. The Dependence versus Independence Dilemma
   with Peter Stromberg   138
8. Kinship Affiliations and Intergenerational
   Relations   163
9. Conclusion   184

References   197

Index   207

Tables

2.1 Sample Characteristics at Time 1   26
3.1 Comparison of Values by Generation   46

vi ◇ Contents

3.2 Relationship Emphasis in the Reorganization
     Process   50

5.1 Changes in Grandparenting   106

6.1 Relationships between Parents and Divorcing
     Children   125

Figure

1.1 Family Structure with Divorce and Remarriage
     Relations   11

PREFACE

THIS book is based on a study of intergenerational relationships during the divorce process. The original objective was to explore how the increasing incidence of divorce was affecting the family status of older people. When the project was designed in the early 1980s, few research findings had been published on grandparenting, and virtually nothing was found in the literature on alterations in grandparenting following divorce. This gap in the literature provided the focus of the research. The important research question was, under what circumstances does the divorce of an adult child serve to further integrate grandparents into their children's families and when does divorce isolate them and deprive them of social supports? Since the divorce process entails reorganization of both the kinship system and the nuclear family, it was also deemed an excellent opportunity to examine intergenerational relationships and how roles of parent and grandparent are redefined.

To pursue these goals, we determined that an intensive descriptive study of a limited number of families would be preferable to a large-scale study testing specific hypotheses. Having selected this general design, it became necessary to control for the variables that account for most differences in family organization, namely, social class and ethnicity. Only white, middle-class families were selected, and those from minority and immigrant groups were excluded. Also, since women are typically more active than men in family activities, our primary focus was the grandmother, although systematic information also was collected on grandfathers and some of them were interviewed.

Most respondents were identified from the public records of San Francisco Bay Area suburbs. We interviewed the divorcing individuals and then went on to interview their parents and others along the divorce and remarriage chains. As the findings emerged, the original focus of the study, the grandparents' role in the divorce process, was overshadowed by the complex dynamics taking place between grandparents and their adult children. As the study progressed, we found that a grandmother's relationship with her adult child was the most important determinant of her grandparenting role. In fact, the factors that influenced these women's life satisfaction and overall sense of well-being had far more to do with their parenting roles than with their grandparenting roles.

The book thus extends far beyond my original focus on grandparenting and includes an examination of relationships among three generations in the extended family system during the dynamic period of family reorganization following divorce. The following chapters will describe how each generation responds to the event of divorce and how these responses ultimately affect the roles of grandparents and their interactions with their children and grandchildren. Since this report has grown out of ongoing research with white, middle-class divorcing families in Northern California suburbs, the findings apply to one segment of the population in one geographic area of the country.

The conceptual framework and research approach come from my background as a social anthropologist whose teaching and research interests have been in family studies and social gerontology. Beginning with dissertation research in the early 1970s, my interests have focused on how family and kinship relationships respond to changing cultural contexts. Original research on intergenerational relationships in Japanese-American and Italian-American families provided insights on more traditional family systems and how they change with each generation in this country. Family relationships in these ethnic groups vary considerably from the families of middle-class, nonethnic America, particularly in the degree of attachment to other family members and the feelings of obligation to conform to family goals.

Such differences became particularly apparent upon studying the social supports of older people in Northern California, most of whom had shed any remnants of ethnic affiliation. For many, the divorce of their children was a source of concern ranking only after worries about their own health and functioning. Since most individuals lacked the supportive extended family often found in ethnic families, both divorces of adult children and the increasing likelihood of declining functioning of the older generation imposed considerable strain on intergenerational relationships. As my interests shifted to more "modern" family types, the study of families in San Francisco suburbs became most appropriate, for these areas are known for their modern or even postmodern life-styles. While not intentional, these research efforts have moved along a continuum that depicts historical changes in the family. In contrast to the relatively structured, obligatory family systems of the past, today's contemporary American family has become more flexible and permissive, permitting individuals much leeway to mold relationships on the basis of their personal preferences. Because individuals in modern families have numerous options, they must continually deal with modern dilemmas arising from the contradictory pull between individual interests and family interests. These dilemmas provide the underlying themes of the book.

This research was made possible by grants from the National Institute of Mental Health and the National Institute on Aging. I am particularly grateful to the staff and reviewers of these agencies, who gave critical advice on the research design at several stages of the grant process. Since 1981, numerous individuals have contributed to this research, either as research associates or as thoughtful advisers and colleagues. In the former category, Barbara Barer worked on all phases of the research through most of these years. Although she was not available in the final stages of data analysis, she made significant contributions as an interviewer, an interpreter, and a colleague. Donald Catalano was an active research associate in the first stages of the research, and Catherine Schmidt performed the same functions in the later wave of interviews. Emily Hancock and Peter Stromberg worked more briefly, but no less productively, as research associates. When the interviews were being planned and, somewhat later, analyzed, George DeVos, Frank Johnson, and Judith Wallerstein provided important insights on the psychodynamic aspects of the data, which only those with clinical background can provide. In the final stages of preparation of this manuscript, Vern Bengtson, Seymour Fisher, and Lillian Troll made many useful suggestions which have resulted in a greatly improved publication. Finally, my deepest gratitude goes to the respondents who shared their lives with us, always in open, articulate discussions. The responsibility for the interpretations, however, is entirely my own.

Portions of this book have been published in somewhat different form in *American Anthropologist* (1988), *The Gerontologist* (1987, 1988), *Journal of Marriage and the Family* (1988), *Research on Aging* (1983), and *Grandparenthood*, V. Bengtson and J. Robertson, eds. (1985).

EX FAMILIA

◇ 1 ◇

INTRODUCTION

TRADITIONALISM and modernism are terms that take on varied meanings. When one thinks of traditionalism in the family, for example, two contradictory visions emerge. One vision of families living by custom and conventions is nostalgic (Taubin and Mudd 1983). In this view, the traditional family is a large extended family whose members value loyalty, share mutual interests and obligations, and work together for continuity and stability in family life. A second vision is a negative one, depicting the family in its traditional form as a repressive institution that inhibits human potential and personal growth. The "modern" family, the model of the fifties, likewise is difficult to define, but in most cases it evokes visions of the nuclear family with a stably married couple who are bound together by emotional attachments and companionship. If one moves farther along a continuum of family types, a new form of the family emerges, which is appropriately labeled the postmodern family form. This unit is flexible and elastic in its form and functions and permissive in its values.

The families studied here tend to cluster at the modern and postmodern end of the continuum. Most have lived all of their lives in California, a region of the country that has long been noted for its widespread and enthusiastic acceptance of new moralities and life-styles. Evidence suggests, however, that this region differs from the rest of the country only in the degree to which changes are accepted (Caplow et al. 1982).

Three demographic changes are affecting the structure and organization of the American family virtually everywhere. First, there have been shifts in the structure of the family and the timing of events in the developmental cycle because of the delayed age of marriage, declining marriage and birth rates, sharply increased divorce rates, increased rates of illegitimacy, and the rise in single-person households. Second, even more pervasive are the marked changes in women's roles. Larger numbers of women work outside the home, among them many mothers of small children. With the high divorce rate, more families are headed by women. Third, there has been a "graying of America" as the average life expectancy increases and the birth rate decreases. In particular, women are living longer than men, thus being widowed and living alone for longer periods of time. In combination, these demographic changes have resulted in more Americans throughout the country spending shorter periods of their lives living in nuclear families. The effects of these demographic changes interact with changing cultural factors in producing new views on sexuality, on female roles, and, in fact, on the family itself.

Despite the antifamilism found in many recent social trends, a majority of the population in the United States still endorses familistic values and exclusivity in marriage (Macklin 1983; Bane 1976). Women may work and couples may divorce, but the nuclear unit continues to be the preferred one. Among industrial democracies, the United States not only has the highest divorce rate but also the highest marriage rate, which suggests that most individuals value marriage as a desirable goal (Laslett 1978). In her book *Here to Stay* (1976), Bane uses demographic evidence to document the strengths and persistence of the nuclear family. Even more convincing is evidence from research in Middletown (Caplow et al. 1982), a midwestern community studied over a fifty-year period. This evidence indicates that even with a higher divorce rate and changing roles of women, the family system itself has shown surprisingly little change in structure and organization. Americans today appear to be particularly concerned about their social attachments.

The authors of *Habits of the Heart* (Bellah et al. 1985) make an overt appeal for the restoration of more traditional values of family and community. The popularity of this book suggests that such a plea has struck a responsive chord with the wider population and perhaps comes at a time in history when reassertion of traditional forms may be in the offing.

Perhaps the reversion to pro-familism is related to the common set of assumptions that individuals' needs are best met by a small unit resembling the nuclear family. Although the nuclear family has been identified as a source of personal unhappiness, it remains the preferred form of most Americans, including a large proportion of the respondents in this study. Consequently, its configuration merits some discussion here (Parsons 1949). The nuclear family, a prototype for the "normal American family," is a small unit consisting of the marital couple and their children who are residentially separated from kin. Ideally, this unit fulfills the primary emotional needs of its members. It should provide a stable setting for parenting of children during the preschool years and for meeting the marital couple's need for intimacy. The nuclear unit is a private entity in which actions within the household are not open to the observation of outsiders (Seeley et al. 1956). In these conceptions, childrearing activities are gradually transferred to schools and other institutions. Thus, women, who are viewed as the primary socialization agents and the emotional stabilizers in the family, have fewer family functions after the intensive activities of raising small children.

Since children are expected to be independent of the family in early adulthood, the conventional nuclear family form lasts a relatively short time in the life cycle. In a middle-class subculture, marriage entails a prominent break with the family of origin. Adult children are expected to maintain a separate residence once they marry and to be economically independent; therefore, most parents have difficulty in accepting an adult child's return to a dependent status. Although in reality parents give considerable financial help, the relationship between parents and their married children should ideally be "intimate at a distance" (Rosenmayr

1972; Sussman 1968). Since the nuclear unit is private, a married child's life is shielded from parental observation and influence. Parents, even when they become grandparents, are privileged guests rather than members of the household (Turner 1970). In all, the conjugal family system places high priority on the marital bond, often at the expense of the intergenerational linkage.

The nuclear unit may be declining in numbers, but despite its many critics, Laslett (1978) has concluded that the nuclear family is "here to stay" because it provides intimate relationships that meet the needs of individuals. This unit also is the primary basis for personal identity (Weigert and Hastings 1977). Because its functions are primarily psychological and emotional, however, there are likely to be intense feelings among family members, which may be a source of tension. Laslett (1978) suggests that these relatively new functions may in part account for the rise in divorce and in rates of conflict and violence among family members.

We can find at least partial explanations for inconsistent views of the family by augmenting survey and demographic data with an analysis of the developmental cycle of specific families. Such an analysis can account for changes in various family forms occurring over each family's history. At any one time, individuals may live in a nuclear family or have that as their goal, but in the natural history of a family today, there is likely to be a progression of forms as a result of marital changes and changing domestic structures. At some points, the structure may fall below the nuclear model because of divorce or widowhood, and at other periods, such as following remarriage, the family may acquire additional members. We observed the families in this study over almost four years and used retrospective accounts from both generations to extend our knowledge of each family's history. Thus, this study provides the opportunity to examine how family organization both reflects and is influenced by widespread cultural changes.

With the prevalence of divorce and remarriage, changes in the family are of such magnitude that new conceptual approaches are needed to analyze families at such stages. Findings reported here come from analysis of data at three levels. First, following the contemporary emphasis in anthropology (Geertz 1973; Schneider 1968), the cultural component is kept distinct from the social dimensions. Here I refer to the beliefs, ideologies, and evaluations individuals assign to their situation, their actions, and their relationships with others. One can then compare cultural evaluations specifically in terms of the norms and values of each generation.

Second, with divorce, the family changes its structure and the positions, status, and roles of its members. The domestic unit is no longer the biological unit or the nuclear unit. With these changes in family structure, individuals redefine their roles and relationships. In most cases, however, the roles individuals play following marital changes no longer have a strong normative component, so individuals must improvise. Role making becomes necessary because previous rights and obligations are no longer prescribed (Aldous 1974; Walker and Messinger 1979).

The third area of analysis focuses on dyadic relationships in the family and how they change with marital changes. Changes in dyadic relationships are depicted using the concept of boundary (Walker and Messinger 1979; Hess and Handel 1967; Troll 1980b), which here refers to "those factors which contribute to the sense of identity differentiating one group from another" (Walker and Messinger 1979, 186). Boundaries may be physical, such as the walls of a house or a locked bedroom door; they may be psychological in that they define the degree of intimacy and closeness between individuals; or they may be social and either distinguish or blur various roles and relationships. This analysis of intergenerational relationships during the divorce process is guided by the assumption that divorce entails the process of restructuring the family and the kinship system. The process is dynamic for both individuals and the social groups in which they live, for the previous structures have broken down with divorce. Walker and Messinger (1979) suggest that marital changes affect boundaries, usually making them more open and permeable. Changes in boundaries also may affect the degree of clarity and continuity in parental roles.

THE CULTURAL CONTENT
OF FAMILY RELATIONSHIPS

The concept of culture is such a vague and variably defined concept that it can be applied to much of social life. For our purposes, however, the concept of culture does not refer to social actions but to the blueprint (Geertz 1973) or "tool kit" that provides the strategies for action (Swidler 1986). Among its dimensions are the beliefs, ideologies, norms and values, and traditions that provide the underpinnings for behavior. In American culture, there is little uniformity in these dimensions of culture. In fact, since a major cultural premise concerns the freedom of individuals to decide their courses of action, individuals play an important role in shaping their own social environment. In contrast to cultures where there are more direct and explicit pressures for social conformity, American culture permits or even encourages individual freedom and flexibility. During periods of uncertainty such as those found in the divorce process, cultural factors are particularly evident (Swidler 1986). Among the interstices of social life where established beliefs and norms either were never evident or are now no longer held, cultural factors more directly influence outcomes.

Even before the steep rise in the divorce rate and the social changes described above, popular critics of American culture expressed concern about the fragility of social ties in American culture. Such expressions, which often border on clichés, are so pervasive that it has become almost prosaic to speak of American culture as producing an independent, individualistic, self-reliant character type who stands relatively aloof from family and community ties. Most often, the analysis of American culture addresses the outcomes of cultural trends in terms of anomie, alienation, and the deterioration of moral values (Barber 1986; Bellah et al. 1985; Lasch 1978; Lasch 1984; Slater 1970). In recent years, these cultural patterns have also been associated with a new American character type. This character resembles neither the emotionally isolated, internally driven, "inner-directed man" nor the conforming, socially attuned "other-directed man" (Riesman, Glazer, and Denney 1950). Ralph Turner (1976) has suggested that the new individual rejects the institutional anchorages of self and is "impulse-directed." Among the dimensions of this character type are the endorsement of pleasure-seeking activities over social responsibilities and expressiveness over insight, a heightened psychological awareness, a shift from future time orientation to the present, and a rejection of pressures for social conformity. Countless labels have been attached to the recent expression of this phenomenon: the culture of narcissism, the new sensibility, self-actualization, or the greening of America. These shifts in culture and character entail, among other things, a liberation from the Victorian ideal of industry and self-reliance (Quinton 1983).

From a review of current commentary and from the first round of data collection in this research, several themes were selected for further study in order to derive concepts that could be measured. First, in recent times there has been a decline in the influence of traditional sources of authority, which in the past were found in family and the community. Numerous causal explanations for this decline have been evoked—economic prosperity, technological changes, permissive childrearing practices, progressive education, or the natural continuity of historical processes. In any case, conservative and liberal evaluations of these trends are consistent with Christopher Lasch's conclusion that individuals have "a life liberated at last from the prying eyes of neighbors, from village prejudices, from the inquisitorial presence of elders, from everything narrow, stifling, petty and conventional" (1984).

Second, with the decline of authority, large numbers of our population have developed pluralistic conceptions of personal freedom. These can be associated with all kinds of panaceas—sexual freedom, open marriages, serial monogamy, or nonbinding commitment (Gans 1974). Also, with the decline of traditional bases of authority and social control, various therapeutic sources of help so popular today have become new forms of control (Lasch 1979). While the new consciousness or new personhood is humanistically based, there are differing views on its impact on individuals. Some critics view the new consciousness as a great step toward personal fulfillment. Others point out that in the process of achieving personal fulfillment the traditional bases of supports and nurturance are undermined (Bellah et al. 1985). In any case, when this value configuration predominates, individuals are less likely to impose their own values, standards of morality, and personal preferences on other family members. Moreover, the family is less likely to transmit moral values.

Third, the dilemma of dependence versus independence is most prominent among those who endorse personal growth and freedom. Family members may disagree on the optimal degree of attachment individuals should have to the primary group, thus raising issues of conflicting interests: dependence versus independence, group interests versus personal interests, and altruism versus self-interest. On the one hand, people are expected to be independent: to stand on their own two feet, to pull themselves up by their own bootstraps, and ad infinitum. This value orientation is so pervasive that it is generally taken for granted in analyzing American character. On the other hand, some critics suggest that these messages to be independent may undermine the family system's capacity to care for the dependent old and young members; they also may affect the society's need for interdependence, which is essential for social stability (Gouldner 1960; Johnson 1985b).

Divorce and the subsequent process of family reorganization throw these values into clear relief. Since the Northern California subculture is noted for the freedom it grants to individuals, relationships can be molded in such a manner that, unlike in the past, onerous obligatory relationships do not have to be grudgingly maintained. In later chapters, I will document the pleasure-seeking, fun-loving ideal of grandparenting and the friendship ideal so often applied to the parent-child relationship. Cultural dimensions centering on personal freedom may also result in family relationships that are voluntary rather than obligatory. Thus, relationships may become more like friendships, and as such, they are optionally maintained on the basis of mutual attraction. The dominant themes of this book, therefore, are how these values regarding family life are translated into the maintenance of on-going family and kinship relationships and how, in the midst of divorce-related changes, individuals deal with the issue of the optimal degree of attachment to family members. The book is about the dilemmas individuals express in the face of the new freedoms the culture permits, freedoms that are enhanced by the very event of divorce.

DIVORCE'S IMPACT
ON FAMILY STRUCTURE

Divorce creates such major rearrangements in the structural units of the family that interpreting these phenomena poses serious definitional problems. It becomes necessary to distinguish between the biological, domestic, and extended family units (Johnson 1988b). The nuclear family has its biological roots in the act of procreation and the care of the dependent infant. It is useful to use this unit as a baseline structure from which to plot changes following divorce and remarriage (Gellner 1957; Gellner 1960). The biological unit is comprised of marital, parent-child, and sibling relationships. Cross-culturally this unit may be difficult to identify, for it can shrink to the mother-child dyad or it may be so submerged in an extended family unit that it is not a functional unit (Adams 1960; Murdock 1949). The biological unit potentially provides the basis for expansion of the kinship unit, as an individual accrues both consanguineal and affinal relatives—the consanguineal relatives of the individual's spouse or parents and the affinal relatives of the individual's children and siblings.

In contrast to the biological unit, in which membership does not necessarily entail common residence or daily interactions, the domestic unit usually functions on a day-to-day basis. The household may or may not include biological or marital relationships. In fact, almost one-quarter of American households include only one individual. Nevertheless, this is the "lived-in family" (Sussman 1985), the unit that usually cooperates in performing the basic functional prerequisites of bearing and rearing children. After marriage and the birth of children, most Americans live in a domestic unit that also is the nuclear family, or the biological unit of procreation. In the American kinship system, membership is often diffusely defined to include those to whom one feels related (Schneider and Cottrell 1975). There are usually two identifiable units. First, the *immediate family* resembles the modified extended family, a unit that usually includes a person's family of orientation and family of procreation. Before marriage, individuals refer to their parents and siblings as their immediate family. With marriage, a spouse and his family of orientation are usually included. Second is an amorphous group of *kindred*. If taken phenomenologically, there is great variation in the depth and density of this unit. The number of individuals identified may simply be a function of the time the interviewer spends with informants and the persistence of the questioning. The extended family system in American culture is by definition bilateral, but this system has a matrilateral focus. Women usually coordinate kinship activities and facilitate the linkage between relatives.

While the biological unit and the domestic unit are usually treated synonymously with the nuclear family, more precise definitions are required for many analytical problems (Bender 1967). The divorcing family is one notable example of how misleading these terms are. When one parent leaves the household, by definition the household becomes abbreviated in its structure. Except in those cases where joint custody is scrupulously observed, one can identify the primary and secondary residences of the children. Other situations are also found, however, when these units are followed over time. Children may change their residence because of

Figure 1.1
Family Structure with Divorce and Remarriage

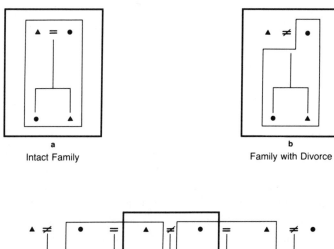

a
Intact Family

b
Family with Divorce

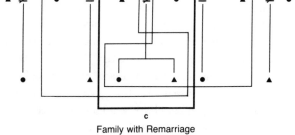

c
Family with Remarriage

Biological Unit ━━━

Domestic/Nuclear Unit ────

▲ = Male

● = Female

conflict with the custodial parent, or they may spend considerable time at their grandparents' residence. Also, commonly one or both parents remarries or forms a nonmarital household. The new partner is likely to have children from a previous marriage, who may or may not have that household as their primary or secondary residence. In all, identifying the household of the children of divorce is fraught with problems during periods of marital changes.

The changes in structure described above usually have a major impact on the organization of the family's roles and activities. Because of the emotional significance of marriage and because the nuclear family's existence rests upon its continuity, marital instability creates particular problems for this family type. With the breakup of the nuclear household, roles change. Dependent children usually have only one parent available on a day-to-day basis. This parent is frequently overburdened in attempting to meet parenting responsibilities of two adults. Divorce also frequently undermines the emotional and physical well-being of both the custodial parent and the children. Significantly higher rates of both physical and mental illness for adults and developmental problems for children are reported following divorce (Longfellow 1979; Wallerstein and Kelly 1979; Weed 1979). Paul Bohannon (1971) has noted that such divorce-related problems only arise in societies such as ours where the household is based upon the marital dyad. In fact, in cultures where kinship bonds commonly are the basis for the household, the marital tie can be in competition with kinship loyalties. In such cases, marital instability usually strengthens the domestic unit and in the process most likely enhances the stability of blood relationships.

In contrast, members of the contemporary nuclear family system are more vulnerable with marital instability because the nuclear unit is only loosely connected to the kinship group. Although recent surveys report that most Americans are in frequent contact with relatives (Adams 1971; Shanas 1979), the nature of this contact is quite different from the corporate nature of kin ties so often found in small-scale societies. Rather than having explicitly defined rights and obligations with kin, the nuclear unit is connected to each spouse's parents and siblings by bonds of affection and sentiment. Given the flexibility and elasticity of this family system (Furstenberg 1981), individuals have the freedom to dissolve both marital and kinship ties. The results, however, are social environments far more complex than those where marriages are stable, because divorce does not necessarily mean that relationships between the formerly married and their relatives end.

Relationships with affinal relatives, which have accrued through one's marriage, are legally dissolved with divorce, but some relaionships continue to have their biological underpinnings. A former spouse remains the parent of one's child. With divorce, one's spouse becomes an ex-spouse and his or her parents become ex-in-laws; nevertheless, they also remain, respectively, "my child's parent" and "my child's grandparents." With marital changes and the freedom to define who one's relatives are, an extended family unit may consist of a network of consanguineal and affinal relatives of whom the latter may come from both marriages and divorces (Johnson and Barer 1987). Operationally, parents with dependent children generally must coordinate their childrearing activities, so their relationship as co-parents to children must continue. While the household may change markedly, the biological unit by most definitions changes less so because of the blood ties each parent retains with the children. The children's conception of the family may differ from that of their parents, for they have membership in two families. The nuclear family of their custodial parent is usually their primary family unit, but they also have some affiliation with the household of their other parent. Either one unit or both are likely to be expanded as new partners of the parents join the household, often with their children by a previous marriage. The extent to which children consider these new members in the nuclear family of a parent as family or kin varies, but, operationally, children of divorced families are likely to be in frequent contact with steprelatives.

In any case, the kinship system potentially is expansive with marital changes as some former in-laws are retained after divorce and new in-laws are added with remarriage. This expansion comes not only from one's own marital changes, but also with the marriages and divorces of consanguineal and affinal relatives. Depending upon one's definition of relationships, the affinals of the remarriage may occupy the gray areas in the kinship charts, even among those who share a household. Is a stepfather equated with a father? Is his daughter equated with a sister? Where personal choices operate, one finds much variation in how the kinship system is used for social purposes. Also, since it is common for Americans to blur distinctions between kin and friends (La Gaipa 1981; Paine 1974), the operational social units of relationships outside the household may vary considerably.

Since grandparents, the parents of the divorcing individuals, are the most stable figures throughout these marital changes, their role also is likely to be expanded with divorce as they come to the aid of their children and grandchildren. The widespread attention devoted to grandparents in the media possibly stems from the hope that they can be a stabilizing force in the contemporary American family. There is some evidence, however, that today's grandparents are quite different from grandparents of the past (Bengtson and Robertson 1985). As their child's family undergoes reorganization following divorce, their potential functions in their children's dissolving families are diverse because this generation of grandparents is younger, healthier, and more financially secure and has large blocks of leisure time. Perhaps for the first time in history, grandparents are freed from other responsibilities to the extent that they can play a key role in the family system. Because there is usually an attrition of roles with aging, positive benefits could come from enlarging the content of the grandparent's role. As old roles are lost, they potentially could be replaced by greater family involvement. Most observers agree that despite the possible benefits to both generations, however, greater involvement is not widespread (Bengston and Robertson 1985).

BOUNDARY CHANGES

Family reorganization after divorce entails redefinitions of relationships both in the nuclear household and in the informal social network of relatives and friends. As the divorcing household breaks down, the shield of privacy around this unit is lowered and individuals' actions are more readily observable to parents and other relatives. By definition, divorce creates cleavages in the nuclear family that affect relationships in the extended family. Over a period of time, after cleavages appear in previous solidarities, processes of reorganization occur in which new solidarities are forged. In these new arrangements, parents vary in the roles they play in their adult children's families. Variations in the patterns of solidarity formed during the reorganization process can be used to form a typology.

Three configurations of family organization were observable in the families we studied. First, some parents and children reemphasized the blood tie between generations after the breakup of the children's marriages. Second, other divorcing parents and their children continued to emphasize the nucleated family: the household was the dominant unit, and parents and relatives were relatively remote. Third, still others formed loosely connected kin networks in which all three generations were included in an amorphous group of consanguineal and affinal relatives as well as former in-laws.

The concept of boundary is used here to analyze these types of solidarities. As discussed previously, the concept here refers to sociological dimensions such as the degree of separateness or connectedness between social units, whether they be households or individuals performing social roles or conducting relationships. Boundaries between units may be flexible, open, and loose, permitting freedom and change, or they may be tightly structured and impermeable, resulting in a unit characterized by stability and immunity from outside influences.

The questions posed here center on how these types of solidarities and the boundaries that enclose them operate in the wider social context and how they change over time. The following suggests how changes in the boundaries between individuals and households occurring in the divorce process are associated with the solidarity between parents and their adult children. For example, if a daughter becomes dependent on her parents following her divorce, the private boundary around her nuclear household will become more permeable. In the process, she has opened up her life to her parents' purview and comment, and it is likely that her parents will have the opportunity to exert more influence over her life. If, however, the boundary around her nuclear unit remains relatively impermeable to her parents, her life will remain private and impervious to parental influence. On the contrary, if she forms a loose-knit, changeable network of relationships, its permeable boundaries will permit the introduction of new norms, which will compete with those of her parents.

Because of the dynamic changes taking place in these families, however, the patterns may be unstable and changeable as individuals adapt to the demands of the post-divorce situation. We will trace these changes and illustrate how patterns of reorganization affect intergenerational relationships. For example, if the generational emphasis is prominent after divorce, I assume that this emphasis is only possible because of long-term solidarity between parent and adult child, which may have been deemphasized during the time the child's nuclear family was intact. Nevertheless, when the divorced adult child's needs decline sometime later, the parents' support for the child may decline, but these resources are available to be recalled if needed. If the divorcée retreats with her children behind the walls of the nuclear family after her divorce and has only superficial relationships with kin, she is reflecting previous patterning of relationships in which social distance has always been maintained with relatives outside the nuclear household. Finally, if divorced individuals are swept along in a dynamic network dominated by a changing cast of previous, current, and even future in-laws, it is likely that these individuals have always been relatively free to construct networks based upon personal preference rather than upon more conventional definitions of the family. In such contexts, individuals are also likely to be exposed to more varied values.

OVERVIEW OF THE BOOK

A description of the methodology appears in the next chapter. Chapter 3 introduces the reader to the cultural context of Northern California suburbs, where divorcing families are struggling with defining and redefining their relationships. In chapter 4, divorce is analyzed as a process that begins with the deterioration of the marriage, continues with the actual breakup of the household, and ends eventually with reorganization. The last stage often entails the formation of new relationships with remarriage.

The remaining chapters will focus on how the divorce process affects family roles and the relationships between generations. Chapter 5 describes the grandmothers and how they define their roles during the divorce process as they respond to the needs of their children and grandchildren. Chapter 6 describes the ripple effect of divorce: how it affects relationships between grandparents and their divorcing children. The case study is used extensively to give descriptive content to the delicate interplay between basic value orientations, more specific normative directives, and the day-to-day interactions between generations. Chapter 7 continues these themes with a discussion of the tensions between parents and adult children, which arise from the contradictory needs to be independent, on the one hand, and to fulfill one's need for relatedness, on the other. Individuals use various mechanisms to reduce these tensions and to carry on relations between generations. Chapter 8 places the respondents' family life into a wider social and cultural framework. The families in the study illustrate most convincingly how the family and kinship systems that form and dissolve with divorce and remarriage represent a relatively new social form. Finally, the concluding chapter reviews the central themes observed in this study of intergenerational relationships in a changing subculture. I discuss the directions of family changes in a white middle-class subculture and the relative costs and benefits of modern family types.

◇ 2 ◇

THE RESEARCH APPROACH

ALTHOUGH the study of the family is of interest to scholars in various disciplines, the literature on the American family is dominated by two approaches. On the one hand, sociologists and social psychologists use valid and reliable instruments to reduce the phenomena under study to measurable dimensions relatively remote from the dramas and emotions of daily family life. On the other hand, clinical researchers study family processes by focusing on these dramas. Clinical studies, however, are often of less use to social scientists because they focus on the motives and feelings of individuals rather than their social context or ongoing social relationships. All these techniques, in any case, must rely on self-report and are subject to problems of social desirability responses. Although the observational methods of anthropology suggest productive insight not forthcoming in other approaches, much of the activity of the American middle-class family goes on behind closed doors, making the standard techniques of participant observation used by anthropologists inappropriate. To get at the contextual or processual aspects of family life yet still meet the scientific standards of social science, it becomes necessary to adapt some form of the interview method and accept the self-reports of the respondents.

In designing this research in the early 1980s, decisions on methods were by no means clear-cut. A review of the literature revealed no study of the grandparents' role in the divorces of their children. It thus became necessary to synthesize three separate areas of research: the effects of divorce on adult children and their parents, the role of grandparents, and the extent to which intergenerational relationships function as a support system during the divorce process. Divorcing parents experience a diminished capacity to parent (Hetherington, Cox, and Cox 1982; Wallerstein and Kelly 1979; Weed 1979). Grandparents could compensate for any parenting deficiencies of their children, but their role is an achieved one that is based more upon personal qualities than upon specific rights and duties. While extended family relationships during the divorce process had not been extensively studied, there was consensus among researchers that American kinship operates in a voluntary and flexible way. A summary of the literature permitted several assumptions. Both divorce and aging are processes in the life cycle where needs for social supports increase. Divorce is increasingly viewed as a process rather than a life event and as a dynamic situation usually involving a restructuring of relationships. This state of flux, or social limbo, in the divorce process is paralleled by relatively open-ended normative conceptions of the grandparent role and of kinship relationships in general.

From both the empirical and theoretical literature, we concluded that divorce results in modifications in relationships between grandparents and their divorcing children and between grandparents and grandchildren. The needs and the demands divorce imposes, we concluded, have a ripple effect on other relationships in the extended family system. We assumed that the previous history of the relationships may or may not be relevant to the changes taking place. We attempted to avoid a problem-oriented approach and made no assumptions as to whether these changes had positive or negative valences.

These conclusions prompted several decisions on research design. First, after several attempts at writing proposals that met the standards of the peer-review process of granting agencies, it became clear that there was insufficient understanding of grandparenting. While the divorce process was well researched, its impact on intergenerational relationships was not. Consequently, any attempts to test hypotheses were abandoned, and the objectives were stated as research questions. With such a study, we were free to follow leads that were productive to our research interests rather than being confined to one type of sample and one research approach.

Second, the projected sample size had to meet two criteria. It had to be relatively small, so those selected could be studied more intensively. The material collected had to be comprehensive enough so each family could be treated as a system in which the interaction of variables could be observed. Yet the sample size also had to be large enough to discern patterns of family reorganization. Through the use of nonparametric statistics, we wanted to determine whether certain findings were idiosyncratic to specific families or a characteristic form of adaptation to divorce.

Third, with these decisions made, the problem of socioeconomic and ethnic variation arose. Since these factors are important sources of family variation, it was necessary to control them and confine the sample to white, middle- and upper-middle-class families who were not members of minority or immigrant groups. By conducting the research in the San Francisco suburbs, an area of the country noted for avant-garde life-styles, we were studying families at one end of a cultural continuum. This has been an advantage because the study of the "tails" of the normal curve, the more extreme expressions of the phenomenon, throws the family processes into clearer relief and thus provides more insight.

Finally, a longitudinal research design was deemed necessary in order to follow family processes over time. In the initial design, plans were made to interview grandparents twice over a one-year period and their divorcing children at our first contact with the grandparents. After this first phase of the research and the observance of family changes over a mean of fourteen months, we found that these families were in a dynamic state of flux because of further marriages and, in some cases, further divorces. These marital changes resulted in reformed kinship systems, many of which became larger and more complex than those found in intact families. Such kinship systems had not been studied in our society by anthropologists, although, at least in their size and complexity, many resembled the kinship systems of small-scale societies.

We decided to continue investigating this sample of divorcing families in order to map family and kinship changes, since we had already collected much information. However, we no longer spoke only of divorce; consistent with the events taking place, we described them as marital changes. With a longitudinal research design, we could plot the status and role of each generation in the new forms of organization that emerged. Another advantage to continuing the research was that the expensive, time-consuming sampling procedures (described below) had already been completed. We also had good rapport with the respondents, many of whom had already invited us to return for more interviews.

In the course of the research, we had an opportunity to consult with Andrew Cherlin and Frank Furstenberg as they prepared an interview instrument for a national follow-up survey. They added some questions we suggested; and for the follow-up interviews, we added some of their questions. Thus, it was possible to evaluate how much the population studied here diverged from the broader population. As a complement to survey research, qualitative studies of a small number of persons and large-scale surveys can mutually inform each other.

SAMPLING

Most of the families were selected from suburban public divorce records. In our selection criteria, we confined potential respondents to white, middle-class individuals who were not members of minority groups. At designated times, we examined all divorces finalized during the previous week. Because financial agreements were part of the records, we were usually able to identify the socio-economic status of the divorced and omit any files that indicated working-class status. These records also had information on the length of the marriage, custody agreements, and the date the formal separation was filed.

We drew only those files where the separation was less than three years, a time frame selected to avoid the bitter acrimony often occurring immediately following the breakup of a household yet ensure that the events were recent enough for effective recall. Sampling was also geared to having roughly equal numbers of maternal and paternal grandmothers and half under sixty-five and half, sixty-five or older. In the first wave of interviewing, our goal was forty-eight families divided more or less equally by age and kinship relationship of the grandmother, so that even with attrition, there would be ten in each cell by our final contact.

After the relevant information was recorded, the arduous process of gaining access to a sample began. Since divorce frequently involves residential changes, the families were difficult to locate. With many unlisted telephone numbers or listings using initials rather than full first names, this task was even more difficult. It often took numerous phone calls to reach the right party. Men were more difficult to locate because they were less likely to remain in the family home. As a result, we began to accumulate more women and their mothers than men and their mothers. In any case, we contacted the first party of divorce we could reach in order to find out if they had either maternal or paternal grandparents in the Bay Area, a region defined as less than one hour by car. In well over half of the families, at least one partner had a parent in the area. Most individuals were initially interested but wanted to discuss the research with their mothers. Some respondents spontaneously encouraged us to call their ex-spouse at that time if he or she met our selection criteria. In most cases, however, the permission to contact the other partner was not secured until the end of the interview. If they resisted, we made no attempt to contact them.

We attempted to study any interesting patterns of reorganization that were reported. For example, if a divorcing man reported that he had less contact with his mother than did his former wife, we attempted to follow this lead. With his permission, we contacted his mother and his ex-wife in order to study in-law coalitions. With such leeway in the research design, we were also able to focus on divorce and remarriage chains in those families that had multiple divorces. In fact, in one case, we followed three generations of divorced women.

However, when most initial interviews were completed, we were still short of paternal grandmothers who were sixty-five years of age and older. Because divorce occurs on the average in the first seven years of marriage, younger divorced families with younger grandmothers are more common. It became necessary to use opportunity sampling to complete this phase of the research on schedule. We advertised in local papers and asked respondents to refer us on to older paternal grandmothers. These efforts brought an adequate response, although at least ten grandmothers volunteered but did not want us to interview their children. We used these women respondents in the analysis of the grandparent role but not in the analysis of the parent-adult child dyad. The latter material came from interviews with members of both generations.

After excluding all of those who did not give us access to their children, we contacted all grandmothers a mean of fourteen months later. By that time, we had lost six grandmothers; one died, two moved away, and three refused to participate. A mean of forty months after the first contact with these families, we again contacted all grandmothers, their divorcing children, and, where relevant, their children-in-law. Some of the grandmothers who had refused to be interviewed at Time 2 consented at Time 3, but a few others refused. In any case, attrition was low in both generations, with four refusals in each generation, three deaths, and two moves over the course of the research. By the third wave of interviewing, only one family did not have at least one member interviewed. The grandparents had died in an automobile accident, and their son refused to be interviewed. In that case, however, his former wife and mother-in-law were participating in the research.

In the following, the numbers in the sample vary depending upon the time of contact to which I am referring. The first two waves of interviews provided in-depth information on fifty-two dyads of grandmothers and their divorcing children, four of which also included interviews with the former child-in-law. In three cases, the only dyad interviewed was the mother-in-law and daughter-in-law dyad because this in-law bond was closer than the parent-child relationship. Of the parent-child dyads, twenty-four were with mothers and daughters and twenty-five were with mothers and sons. Over the forty months the families were followed, we were able to retain forty-three dyads in which both the grandmother and her divorcing child were both interviewed.

SAMPLE CHARACTERISTICS

Table 2.1 summarizes the major characteristics of the sample. The mean age of the grandmothers was 64.2, while their children's mean age was 36.5. Although not listed in the table, the grandchildren's mean age was 11.4. Over two-thirds of the grandmothers were married, and 21 percent of their children had already remarried or were cohabiting by the time we interviewed them. By design, the sample was predominately middle class, although a few respondents were of upper-class or working-class status. Almost half of the divorcing generation had a college or advanced degree, and only 10 percent had not gone to college. The grandparents' situation was reversed; almost half had no college education, and less than one-quarter had a college or advanced degree.

In the divorcing generation, their marriages had lasted a mean of 11.2 years; they had been separated a mean of 2.1 years by the first interview; and there was a mean of 1.9 children in each family. Legally a large portion of the sample had joint custody, but almost two-thirds of the children lived with their mothers. Over one-fourth lived with their fathers or alternated between households.

While not shown in tabular form, the sample is roughly divided among the major religious groups with the exception of the 22 percent who professed no religious affiliation. Consistent with the economic strains after divorce, 87 percent of the divorcing women were working in comparison to 89 percent of the men.

Table 2.1
Sample Characteristics at Time 1

Parent–Adult Child Dyads (N = 52)		
	Grandparents	*Adult Children*
Age means	64.2	36.5
	(by percentage)	
Marital status		
Married	67	21
Divorced	15	79
Widowed	18	0
Education		
Post-college	3	15
College degree	20	33
Some college	30	42
High school or less	47	10
Social Class		
Upper class	8	10
Upper middle class	33	37
Lower middle class	43	46
Working class	10	8

Divorcing Families		
Mean length of marriage		11.2 years
Mean length of time since separation		2.1 years
Mean number of children		1.9
Child's status (by percentage)	*Legal Custody*	*Residence*
Maternal	42	63
Paternal	6	10
Joint	38	17
Undetermined/adult	14	10

Over half of the divorced lived near their former spouse, and where grandmothers were present, they, too, were likely to live in proximity. Most of the grandmothers were in good health and less than one-third were working.

By our second contact, 47 percent of the grandmothers had kinship extensions resulting from their children's marital changes, and this proportion increased by the third contact. Although the time since an adult child's separation had been relatively brief, divorce and remarriage chains were apparent. In the fifty-two kinship systems examined at Time 2, there had been a total of seventy-four divorces at the second generation (adult child) level and twenty remarriages. At least five respondents were cohabiting. The majority of these new partners had also been divorced, and many had children, so there was already a complex array of relationships. The grandparent generation had also experienced divorce. Of the fifty-nine women initially interviewed, ten had been divorced; after either divorce or widowhood, seven were in their second marriage and two were in their third marriage. Obviously, in these unions they also had acquired new stepchildren and stepgrandchildren. Also, 35 percent of the grandmothers had more than one divorced child, so changes in kin relationships were even more far-reaching. By our second contact, seven more adult children and one grandparent had remarried. By the third contact, there were nine additional divorces among grandparents and all of their children and twenty-one additional remarriages. In fact, the situation was a dynamic one for all families, since further marriages and divorces initiated additional formations and breakdowns of affinal relationships, thus opening up a host of potential new relationships at the same time relationships with former in-laws were retained.

THE INTERVIEW FORMAT

With the exception of objective measures of social contact and aid, the interview format was designed to gather qualitative data concerning family life. The interview guide allowed respondents considerable leeway in determining the course of discussion. At the end of each interview, systematic data collection took place to provide an additional reliable source of data.

Conceptually, we have used three levels of analysis: (1) cultural directives, as expressed in norms and values, (2) family structure and the organization of roles, and (3) family relationships and the nature of the boundaries between them. Dimensions of these concepts were used to design the interview format, and the responses were later coded and reduced to measures.

First, the measurable dimensions of the cultural content include value orientations, which we explored through direct questioning and projective story analysis. Value orientations of interest here ranged from the nature of the individual's responsibility to the family to attitudes toward marriage and sexuality. To tap the culture directives of the respondents, interviewers described common situations occurring with divorce when choices had to be made; for example, situations in which individuals had to decide whether to put their personal happiness above family responsibilities or whether to have a lover stay all night when their children were in the household. Grandmothers also responded to the stories, so their values could also be measured and compared to their adult children's values.

Second, to study family roles, the interviewers focused on the congruence between individuals' expectations for their own roles and the roles of other family members and their actual performance of these roles. For example, grandmothers were asked what they expected to do for their children and grandchildren, what they were actually doing for them, and how they felt about what they were doing. In such analyses, those whose role performance was not meeting their expectations could be identified and compared to those whose roles were compatible with their wishes. All respondents were asked to discuss whether grandparents should get involved with their children's problems. (Should a grandmother get involved if a son is drinking too much or if a son-in-law takes grandchildren to his girl friend's house for the night?) To examine the actions of individuals, we used an inventory of social supports potentially exchanged between generations. We also asked to whom individuals would go if they needed help—for example, if they were sick, feeling blue, or just wanted to have some fun.

The analysis of dyadic relationships captured the dynamic aspects of ongoing interactions between grandparents, parents, and children. When this portion of data collection was expanded to examine their transactions with the host of step and in-law relationships acquired or lost by marital changes, many confusions resulted. Both practical and conceptual problems arose because these emerging family forms had rarely been studied. Even American kinship terminology provided no help in understanding these relationships. Relationships were only clarified by establishing a common frame of reference, which distinguished generation levels and relatives related by blood, by divorce, and by remarriage.

G1 The grandparent generation—the parents of the divorcing respondents and the parents of former and present children-in-law (DIG1 and RIG1).

G2 Divorcing parent generation—the parents of the grandchildren and the children of G1 as well as former and present spouses (DIG2 and RIG2).

G3 Children in divorcing families—the grandchildren of G1 and children by other marriages (DIG3 and RIG3).

At each generation level, a series of potential relationships occurred because of marital changes. For example, a grandparent usually had relationships with a new daughter-in-law as well as a former daughter-in-law and with any children either one had from other marriages. Although few formed close relationships with the new or previous spouse's relatives from other marriages, the potential for such relationships was there and thus one we had to explore.

In the analysis of the parent-adult child dyad, attributes of relationships on which we focused included (1) power relationships and the fluctuations in the hierarchy between generations; (2) dependency relationships and any reversals that took place in the divorce process; (3) the give-and-take in their relationship and whether exchanges were voluntary or obligatory and equitable or inequitable; and (4) fluctuations in qualitative dimensions of relationships such as between conflict and consensus or intimacy and distance.

In addition to open-ended discussions, we used other techniques to study relationships. To elicit subjective notions of closeness and distance, we asked individuals to write the names of people in their networks on various concentric circles radiating out from ego. In addition to using multiple techniques of questioning, we obtained information on these families through multiple contacts. Comments in earlier interviews were incorporated into a pen-and-paper questionnaire, so the responses from both techniques could be later compared to other responses. A depression scale, the CES-D, was also used at the final contact.

DATA ANALYSIS

Because of the open-ended nature of the interviews, data analysis was a time-consuming process. Data were coded and reduced to measurement so that dominant patterns and statistically significant variations could be identified. After at least one-half of the interviews were completed, and following extensive discussions with those who had conducted interviews, we prepared a codebook. Then each interview was coded by two individuals. Whenever they disagreed on more than 20 percent of the items, they returned to the interview notes to examine the responses. When no consensus could be reached, the individual who had conducted the interview made the final decision. The same coding categories were used in follow-up interviews so changes could be analyzed.

Case studies and anecdotal material were selected to represent various types of situations and patterns of family reorganization. Because of the small sample, tabular reports are kept to a minimum here and narrative information from the case studies has been used to permit the respondents to speak for themselves.

◇   ◇   ◇

To summarize, both phenomenological and behavioral data are presented. These include not only observable behavior and accounts of behavior but also accounts of the meanings of behavior. Here the analysis encompasses dimensions of the cultural setting in which the research took place, mainly the norms and values that provided the program for action. This program is not only observable in the reports of the respondents but also is reflected in numerous dimensions of their life-styles. The values concern the more global conceptions of what is desirable and the norms are the more specific expectations on the "shoulds" of human interaction.

With such material, there is always a risk of exaggerating the more interesting aspects of these families, those that already form the basis of stereotypes commonly viewed in the mass media. To avoid such risks, I have attempted to select case studies that portray various contrasting patterns and to provide statistical findings to indicate the frequency occurrence for each form. These more systematic tools of social science research and ethnographic representations suggest that the sample used in this research portrays a modern and sometimes exaggerated form of the American family but one that is found in less pronounced forms throughout the country.

◊ 3 ◊

CULTURAL DIRECTIVES AND
INTERGENERATIONAL RELATIONS

CULTURAL factors—beliefs, values, and ideologies—provide the blueprint, or program, by which individuals interpret their experiences and give meaning to their lives (Geertz 1973). Because conceptions are not always consistent with the actual course of events as individuals act out their roles and conduct their social relationships, they need to be considered separately from social phenomena. During periods of change particularly, discontinuities occur between the cultural content and social actions. The divorce process is one such period. Divorce creates upheavals in individuals' lives and, subsequently, inconsistencies between what individuals believe or desire and what they often must settle for. Not surprisingly, then, we find more uniformity in our respondents' beliefs and ideologies than in their actions as they adapt to changes after divorce.

After discussing the cultural directives of our respondents, we will examine how their conceptions are actually translated into actions. The divorcing respondents most prominently differ from their parents in their basic ideas regarding self and family, not only because of age and cohort differences and differing cultural experiences, but also because of the drama of the recent events surrounding divorce. Since this process of redefining roles and relationships often clashes with their parents' conceptions, it merits attention. After reporting upon the cultural material, the chapter concludes with an analysis of varying types of solidarities that form in the process.

CHANGING GOALS AND PRIORITIES
OF THE DIVORCED

Invariably the divorcing parents in this study had modern and permissive values. Most importantly, they endorsed cultural relativity and avoided values that might impose uniform standards of behavior. Most values were acceptable as long as the individuals felt good about them at the time. In fact, few individuals in this project took strong stands on moral values, and even fewer attempted to impose their own views on others. One divorcing man summarized his values in a fairly typical manner: "We all have our values and must face the outcomes. We screen out values which don't suit us. I have basic moral values, but they are subject to change. I question what goes on. Everybody does, but unless you're a Mormon or in some other strict environment, you don't have to follow the strict, old-fashioned stuff, and you shouldn't try to influence others." As the following will suggest, irrespective of the respondents' actions, they favored values centered on the quest for self-fulfillment, sexual freedom, and the effective management of their interpersonal relationships.

Most divorcing respondents had explicit ideas on the components of a good life, most of which differ considerably from the conventional ideals of the 1950s. Their goals were flexible and situationally defined. The comfortable home in the suburbs, a position of prestige and respect in the community, and creative, achieving children were desirable only as long as they brought happiness and contentment. Thus, their conceptions of a good life were existential and centered on the functioning of their internal state. Emphasis on internal experiences and concern for their own happiness, peace of mind, and "no hassles" were often considered the necessary ingredients for family success. Thus, in their minds, family functioning rested upon the internal well-being of the parents. "My children can't do well or be happy unless I am happy" was one of the more overt expressions of such goals. Reportedly, these views were reinforced by psychotherapists in the community, many of whom advised patients that they had to think of themselves first before their family's interests could be served.

Most respondents had clear psychological guidelines for overcoming the travails of divorce and succeeding in their search for happiness. The popular psychological theories, however, did not stem from the Freudian psychology that had influenced their parents in their childrearing practices. Their own parents, on the whole, were quite modern in their views and had used psychological childrearing techniques, so most of these divorced individuals had not been subject to repressive controls commonly found in more traditional families. Although liberated from these repressions, many in the younger generation continued to be preoccupied with their internal psychological processes.

In discussions of their lives and future goals, the divorcing generation usually prefaced their remarks with some expression of the concept of self—self-fulfillment, self-realization, self-actualization, and self-absorption. In some cases, this high investment in one's own internal state came at the expense of career advancement. New life-styles often replaced the older strivings. For example, one man in his thirties gave up a promising career to become a gardener because he concluded that regular work hours would interfere with his self-improvement efforts. Another young man gave up a well-paying job because "I was beginning to want things." In fact, the California state legislature has attracted attention for establishing a $750,000 task force to address social ills by enhancing self-esteem. At the first public meeting, one of the founders of the movement reported, "I believe it is time we unlock inner space in human development and truly become healthy human beings" (*San Francisco Chronicle*, March 5, 1988, p. 1).

Some discussions suggest that introspective concerns had replaced the goal of self-direction and mastery. The aura of Karma was often loosely applied to events over which they felt they had no control: "The day after I bought a house, I lost my job. My Karma was off." Nevertheless, to be psychologically advanced was

a goal for most of these individuals—"to be happy with myself"
or "to be a whole person." In some cases, psychics or "spiritual
healers" assisted in attaining this goal. Family interests on occasion
took a back seat to self-actualization.

This value relativity, which often accompanied self-actualization
strivings, included sexual freedom. Very few of the divorcing
individuals were opposed to living together without marriage. In
fact, most felt that cohabitation was an essential prerequisite to any
possible future marriage. As one man commented, "It takes a long
time for the barriers to come down." Extramarital affairs were not
widely endorsed, however, although many had had open marriages. Sexual permissiveness in many cases was also carried over
to children. Few voiced vehement objections to sexual intimacy
among teenagers as long as the individuals were responsible, here
meaning they were using birth control.

Divorcing parents were able to speak openly to their children
about sex, and teenagers often discussed their first sexual experiences with them. The schools the children attended also took sex
education seriously. In one suburb, several full days were set aside
each year for junior high school students to meet in small groups
in their homes to discuss sex. Children were accustomed to observing their parents' relationships with a series of sexual partners. On
occasion, children sat in on our interviews and openly told their
version of their parents' affairs. Adult children sometimes double-
dated with a parent. After such an occasion, one divorced lawyer
and his college-age son took their dates back to the father's condominium and went off to their respective bedrooms for the night.
In those instances where grandparents and other members of the
family disapproved of what they referred to as "open visiting," few
observers felt it was possible to impose their own moralities on
others. As with most sexual matters, other family members did
not want to be aware of what was going on. Grandparents did not
want to hear about a daughter's abortion. A husband did not want
to know about his wife's casual infidelities. Teenage sexual activity
was viewed as a normal component of the youth culture and thus

impossible to change, so most parents attempted to ignore such activity.

Nevertheless, there appeared to be swings in the pendulum. In interviews, some of the children in these divorcing families, as well as their parents, expressed more traditional values. For example, one divorcing woman in her mid-forties related her many activities of the sixties while raising her children. She and her former husband had been active in the drug revolution, the Summer of Love, and the peace movement. They had lived in numerous communal households, and for one year she had left her family and traveled around the world. To her surprise and dismay now, some years later, there was an abrupt reversal in her daughter, who had become active politically in the Republican party and was on the fringes of the moral majority. And the most surprising change, she found, was in regard to sex. When her daughter and her boyfriend decided to have sex, they became formally engaged and preceded the consummation of the relationship by going to a counselor.

Many respondents expressed ambivalence about their relationships. Their discussions conveyed swings between approach and withdrawal or establishing relationships yet not becoming overly involved with others. In replacing more traditional types of attachments in the family, networks of friends and helping professionals became important sources of advice and assistance. Individuals invested much energy in developing and preserving their networks of meaningful relationships. Such efforts invariably involved study and self-improvement. Respondents usually referred to a romantic relationship as "being in a relationship" rather than having a relationship. According to this ideology, all types of intimate relationships should be "rounded out"; that is, feelings should be out in the open so they can be discussed. Courses were being offered in these suburban areas on how not to be a victim in relationships. Relationships should also be "completed," evidently meaning they should be open to mutual scrutiny and understanding, and nothing should be repressed or left undiscussed. And partners in relationships should be "grounded"—meaning that they should attempt to keep each other stable. The respondents who were particularly concerned with their relationships generally sought out friends and lovers whom they considered psychologically advanced.

Transactional analysis and other therapies helped some of these individuals learn how to negotiate with people. In fact, such an emphasis can start early; we were told of one transactional analysis book designed for seven year olds. Relationships were frequently discussed as being an objective entity divorced from the participants. One mother told us her ten-year-old daughter, when told her mother's relationship with her boyfriend was "breaking down," equated it with a car that breaks down but can be taken to a garage for repair. Self-understanding was usually viewed as a necessary prerequisite for satisfactory relationships. One man reported: "I will see more of my parents when I have room to deal with them emotionally. Now I need no one because I feel good about myself." Others singled out those who were "est people" (Erhard Seminar Training) and those who were not by the way they dealt with their emotions. Spiritual healers or psychics also assisted respondents in reaching higher stages of development. It was believed that to achieve self-understanding, an individual needed freedom, time, and space. Upon the successful completion of this task, when one finally belonged to oneself and no one else, more gratifying relationships were expected to follow. Here is how one divorcing woman described her primary concerns: "I've done a whole lot of growing after years of stagnation. I am making up for lost time. In my marriage, I had sorta given up working on myself. I had my family to think of—there was nothing left for me. What a sacrifice! Now I'm doing only for myself. After I've completed that, I'll be ready to turn to others." Others described fears about being emotionally depleted if they became too close to others. The implication was that they had a finite reservoir of emotions, which had to be carefully parceled out.

Most divorced individuals reported that their chances of achieving a good life improved with their divorce. Only a few people expressed serious regrets, including one woman, who commented: "Deep down, I feel like a loser. I gave him my best years and it was all for nothing." Probably such feelings were rare because the subculture encourages individuals "to work on themselves" and use the divorce as a catalyst for self-improvement.

Even with the importance attached to interpersonal relationships, personal growth was often viewed as having to take place with some modicum of privacy and distance from others. "Space" was the word most frequently used to refer to that ingredient of privacy necessary for equanimity. The majority was attempting to avoid intense heterosexual relationships: "I have a boyfriend, but I am not ready for that to get heavy. Men get too possessive—they move too fast. I want to be alone." One man concluded: "Life is definitely better. I've gotten in touch with my feelings. I don't have to put up with all that bullshit anymore." Another man described his divorce as "like having five thousand pounds off my shoulders." In his new relationship, he was wary of becoming too close and told his lover, "We should slow down and sit back, so we can see where the relationship is going." A woman also felt she needed more solitude: "I am into too many activities. I have to trim down my life. I need more solitude to deal with my new feelings of wholeness."

In other cases, individuals found nonconventional sources of help. One woman described her new significant other: "I have a close friendship with a man in Oregon. We've only been together a few times, but we write a lot. It is a spiritual relationship—he is older, a philosopher—like a spiritual father to me." Sometimes other sources were consulted. When his relationship was not going well, one man consulted an astrologer. He commented, "I learned one thing—stay away from Libras." Another woman described her actions: "I looked in the mirror and said, 'Laura, get your shit together.' I joined a women's group and took a divorce survival course."

Others described themselves as leading "a floating life," a condition that sometimes referred to marital change. In a particularly extreme example, a woman described her three marriages in such a "floating life."

> My first marriage lasted six years—to a chemist I met at a fraternity party. I was pregnant. My next relationship was a nomadic one—we went on the road, leaving our respective children behind. Finally we got married and went home. That lasted five years. Then I married another guy for his dental plan. My teeth were a mess, and I didn't have money to have them fixed. That lasted two years.

A divorced father said his divorce had had no visible effects on his kids, because "marriage is no big deal. For me it was years of mental agony. We weren't role models for the kids for there was no love between us. For them it was better to see me with my lover to see how relationships should be—without all the trappings of marriage." Low expectations for relationships are also evident in the following description of an affair: "It's been an off-again and on-again affair, but now it is on an even keel. We don't do much and we don't share a lot of our lives. We don't go out. We spend most of our time in bed watching TV and making love. We don't talk much, but the relationship suits me. It's relaxing."

STEMMING THE TIDE

The patterning of these cultural factors, we will see in the following, is associated with the type of reorganization in the family taking place after divorce. Before discussing these processes, it must be pointed out that the values described above suggest that a large proportion of the divorcing generation espouse liberal values. There was far more variation in the actual lives of these individuals, however, in part because many individuals were swept along with the ideology of the subculture, sometimes against their will. When their marriage ended, they saw themselves as victims of events over which they had no control.

One example is Sue, a divorced woman in her late thirties with a fifteen-year-old son and a ten-year-old daughter. Sue responded to our questions on values along with the majority. For example, she did not object to sexual freedom for her children because she felt there was nothing she could do about it. When her daughter is older, she plans to provide her with birth control information. Throughout her discussions, her lip service to modern values only superficially overlaid quite traditional values on the family. Much to her distress, however, she had been unable to translate her values into a stable family life and a marriage that would provide the best environment to raise children. Events over which she had little control had changed the course of her life. She had fallen in love with a high school sweetheart. A few years after graduation, just as a large wedding was being planned, he was killed in an automobile accident. She had later married one of his friends and had a satisfactory marriage until her husband began to have affairs. She described her feelings.

> I never asked to be divorced. I thought we had a happy marriage until my daughter told me she saw Daddy with another woman. I tried everything to save the marriage. We went into therapy. He would move out, but I would take him back. It took place over three years—long enough for him to have three affairs. Finally I filed for the divorce.
>
> It's tough being a single parent. I have to sell my house next year. I have to pay everything except a little bit of alimony and child support. And it is written in the agreement that the alimony will stop if I have an affair or even sexual intercourse. I get lonely. I do go to lots of lectures on parenting. I go to therapy twice a week. I try to do the best I can as a mother, but the children feel abandoned by their father and need all sorts of help.

By our last contact, Sue had moved from a spacious house to a small condominium. She was barely able to make ends meet on her salary as a secretary. Her greatest problem was her son, who had developed a serious drug problem. He had been placed in a residential drug rehabilitation program at the cost of five thousand dollars a month, expenses for which she was responsible. She was forced to take out a second mortgage on her condominium, after her ex-husband refused to help. Desperate for financial assistance so her son could stay in the residential drug-treatment program, she reported: "I wrote everyone locally, the state, the federal government. I even wrote Nancy Reagan, but she never responded. I think she was out of the country."

The real insult to her mothering came when, upon her son's release, he moved in with her ex-husband instead of going home. In her mind, her family was attributing this action to her failure to maintain a stable family life. She concluded her interview by saying: "I didn't choose to be a single parent. I didn't choose not to complete my marriage. I have no one. My whole life has backfired." Her commitment to her children nevertheless remained strong. She had ruled out remarriage because it would complicate raising children—"I take parenting seriously and I really believe in until death do us part."

Men also can be swept along by events over which they have no control. For example, Bill was a banker who had accumulated much wealth through real-estate investments. He met his former wife while in college, and they married while he was in graduate school. Both sets of parents were delighted with the marriage because of their common social background. When Sally, his wife, became pregnant, she dropped out of law school. They went on to have two children, ages twenty and fourteen. He described the breakup of his marriage:

> Our problems had been brewing for years. I even avoided my parents so they wouldn't see how miserable I was. Over the years our lives took separate courses. We didn't develop together. The first problem was she didn't like my friends in the business community—she wanted nothing to do with my work. Then she

didn't feel fulfilled and began to look for sources of fulfillment other than in marriage. She became a student of Tai Chi and finally a teacher. She began a relationship with someone there. It was an open one for all to observe. I could see it was powerful and strong. I couldn't live with an open marriage as she wanted to do. So we drew straws, and she divorced me. It wasn't the usual divorce with blood flowing from every orifice. We still meet and are friendly.

Despite this dispassionate description, Bill appeared to be lonely and depressed, reporting, "I still haven't found my bearings." He said that he had only one friend: "an ear brother," a divorced neighbor. He became much closer to his parents, however, after having gone to est in order to "open the door to my family." He also was looking for a new therapist. He was dating, but had not found a significant relationship at our first contact. "My relationships are off-again, on-again. Someone lived here for a while, but she moved out. She wanted children and I didn't want to start a new family." In response to our questions about marriage, he replied: "I believe that marriage is invented to provide a stable environment in which to raise children. When that ceases to be needed, the marriage is completed. If it doesn't work, let there be room for personal growth."

Bill refused our request for another interview, but we did learn from his mother that he had had several unsuccessful love affairs but finally appeared to be in love with a woman who reciprocated his affection. His children were rebelling against their step-father, so he was buying a home in order to accommodate them. His relationship with his parents remained strong.

GRANDPARENTS' CONCEPTIONS OF THE NEW SENSIBILITIES

Since most grandparents attempted to maintain a noninterfering stance, they commonly did not want to be informed about the sexual activities of their children and grandchildren. Many grand-parents reported that they had relaxed their views on living to-gether without marriage, concluding it might be a practical means to avoid another unsuccessful marriage. Most individuals in the older generation, however, would agree with one grandmother: "I'm not thrilled with the open visiting. I don't want my grand-daughter to see her mommy in bed with different men every night. If she does that, she should be sneaky about it." Most grandmothers also were concerned with other aspects of life-style, such as the new religions or consciousness-raising movements. They commonly reported their dismay when their children took est and then "started speaking that psychobabble jargon." Some referred to the "flakiness" of their children and children-in-law: "I worry about my grandchildren. My daughter-in-law has gone through so many stages. It began when they were married by her yoga instructor. No family was permitted. For a long time they slept on the floor, a no-salt diet, no refined sugar. At one point, she got the children up at six to meditate and chant Tibetan words. Her far-out ideas are kooky from my point of view."

Other grandmothers worried about the control some religions had over their grandchildren's minds. For example, when a daughter-in-law joined a religious sect, the Church of Psychic Unity, and sent her grandchildren to the Camp for Integral Studies, the grandmother stood by helplessly. She described her granddaughters as affected by psychic healing, meditation, and too much concern with their "aura." "Those religious fanatics try to put a bubble around their minds so others won't get into their private space—it's a cop out." One grandmother reported with relief, "My son is leading sort of a hippy life, but at least he is wearing shoes to work now." Another described the progression of her son: "I think my son is stuck in the sixties. He doesn't want to be hassled by anything. At school, he used to be a clothes horse—dressed up all the time. But after high school graduation, he started shopping at St. Vincent de Paul and not caring about his appearance. Now he is living with a woman six years older than he—way up in the mountains. We never visit them—we're too afraid of what we would find."

Other grandparents think wistfully of how their children should live. One woman, whose children were on the fringes of the arts and the academic world, commented: "All of my children have lived at the poverty level—damn set on it, first out of choice and then out of necessity. I think back on the time my son used to live in a fairly decent house. He wore a suit every day and took the ferry into the city to work. Then he started looking for his Karma or whatever they call it." Nevertheless, like the average parent in the area, she kept her opinions to herself and voiced values that were more in line with those of her children. Consequently, in many conceptions of the good life, there were few overt disagreements between generations.

As members of this subculture, most grandmothers respected the autonomy and privacy of their children's lives. Thus, they were hesitant to impose their own views on their children, although they were not hesitant to discuss them with us. As I suggested in the introduction, these cultural patterns typify one end of a continuum of values and social character types. In contrast to the views of the divorced generation on family relationships, members of the grandparent generation usually had quite different views of family roles. One grandmother's discussion is fairly typical.

I was the kind of mother—I felt I had to be there all the time. I never worked. I always kept them clean and helped them with their studies. I was active in the PTA. They were never ashamed of me, and they liked my being active in their lives. They had an orderly life. They had to be home on time. They knew dinner would be ready. They knew the rules—I didn't have to discipline sharply. I always got them up for school. I made a good breakfast.

My daughter does none of that. She is not up when they go to school even when she is working. The house is a mess—all the dishes are in the sink. No one cleans up the kitty litter, so the place smells. No one remembers whether the children had their shots. They have free run—no hours or supervision. They hear and see all those things going on that children shouldn't see.

Nevertheless very few grandmothers would intervene. In our second contact, the grandparents were asked their opinion on a woman who in the quest for personal happiness wanted to leave her husband and children. Only one-third of the grandparents openly condemned her; most felt she had a unilateral right to leave or at least had the right to negotiate a compromise with her husband. In fact, as will be described in the following, most grandparents felt that their primary responsibility as grandparents was to avoid imposing their values on their children. In the words of one, "I go by the rules my kids make. I probably just uphold the standards they set for their children. It's best not to say what is right or wrong."

GENERATIONAL DIFFERENCES IN CULTURAL DIMENSIONS

Most members of the grandparent generation dismissed searches for self-actualization as selfishness typical of the "me" generation. These patterns of self-absorption colored their relationships with their children at least indirectly. In addition to open-ended discussions on values, we used projective story techniques to tap changes in sexual morality and the respondents' values on the proper balance between personal interests and family interests. One story concerned a middle-aged man who fell in love with a young woman and insisted upon divorcing his wife of twenty-five years. His justification was that he would be miserable if he did not marry the young woman. When asked if he had the right to do so, almost half of the grandparents but only 18 percent of their children disapproved of his demands (see table 3.1).

A second story elicited less difference in the views between generations: A grandmother faces the choice of taking her first trip to Europe or using the money instead to finance her granddaughter's first year at Stanford. Only 11 percent of the children felt she should give up the trip, while 29 percent of the grandparents agreed this sacrifice was appropriate. It would seem, then, that

Table 3.1
Comparison of Values by Generation
$N = 46$ parent–adult child dyads[a]
(by percentage)

	Parents	Adult Children
Divorce for personal happiness		
Approve	32	52
Unsure	19	31
Disapprove	49	18*
Grandmother give up her trip		
She should not	40	54
Compromise	31	35
She should	29	11*
Cohabitation to retain alimony		
Approve	30	37
Under some circumstances	22	13
Disapprove	48	50*
Cohabitation		
Approve	38	82
Under some circumstances	36	13
Disapprove	26	5*
Extramarital Affairs		
Approve	7	20
Disapprove	93	80*
Teenagers having sex		
No objection	35	73
Disapprove	65	27*
Divorce as a growth experience		
Agree	26	71
Disagree	74	29*
A woman's first duty is		
To herself	47	82
To her family	53	18*

*$p < .05$
[a]N varies because questions were asked at two points in time.

personal freedom and self-actualization were stronger concerns for the younger generation, though the grandparents had also been influenced by these new values. In principle they may have felt that a man has no right to sacrifice his family in the interests of his own happiness, but as grandparents they also felt they should not have to sacrifice for their children and grandchildren. In matters of morality, there were even fewer differences between generations. Another story described a situation in which a woman with latency-age children lived with a man she loved. This option was selected, respondents were told, so she would not lose her alimony. In their responses, half in each generation disapproved of such a situation.

Projective stories depicting hypothetical situations did not elicit as many differences between generations as did direct questioning, perhaps because their own concerns were more immediate than were the hypothetical situations of strangers. In our last round of interviewing, we directly asked respondents about their views on the new moralities. The findings (see table 3.1) reveal significant differences between generations. First, almost all of the divorcing generation approved of couples living together without marriage, in contrast to only 38 percent of the grandparents. In response to a question on their approval of teenagers having sexual relations "before they are old enough to vote," almost three-quarters of divorcing parents voiced no objection in comparison to 35 percent of the grandparents. Although divorced individuals were less likely to disapprove of extramarital affairs, neither generation approved of these arrangements.

The generations also differed in their values on self-fulfillment. For example, almost three times as many divorced parents as grandparents agreed that divorce was a "growth experience." In fact, grandparents objected to equating divorce with growth, occasionally calling it a "gross experience." When questioned directly about the ordering of women's priorities, nearly twice as many of the divorced generation said a woman's first responsibility was to herself rather than to her family. In all, these variations reveal striking differences in values between generations.

When correlations were run to identify any significant associations with liberal attitudes, there were only two significant findings among the grandparents. Those grandmothers who approved of sexual freedom were less likely to attend church and were less likely to change their patterns of contact with their children—they neither increased nor decreased contact after the divorce. It is possible that, at least in regard to sexual freedom, grandparents who espouse flexible values have relationships with their adult children that do not change with divorce.

These values on sexual behaviors were more significantly associated with family patterns among their divorcing children. Correlations run with this group suggest that liberal values on sexual behavior are inversely associated with their relationship with their parents. Those who had liberal attitudes had a more distant and conflictual relationship with parents than those who were more conservative. Individuals who espoused sexual freedom also were more likely to form flexible networks after divorce that included present and past in-laws. Also, those who agreed that divorce was a growth experience were more likely to maintain friendly relations with former in-laws.

CULTURAL FACTORS AND
THE REORGANIZATION OF
INTERGENERATIONAL RELATIONS

The above findings suggest there are striking value differences between generations, differences that are most likely associated with the quality of the parent-adult child relationship following the child's divorce. Parents differed in the roles they played in their adult children's families during the divorce process and the reorganization of the kinship system. As noted in the introduction, this variation was observable in the nature of the boundaries that defined the degree of separateness or connectedness between social units, for example, between households or between their relationships with each other. Boundaries between units may be flexible, open, and loosely bound, permitting freedom and change, or they may be tightly structured and impermeable, resulting in a unit characterized by stability and immunity from outside influences.

To understand the meanings of changes in some relationships in contrast to stability in others, categories were formed on the basis of the patterning of solidarities observed in the post-divorce family. Once these patterns were identified, we could examine the interaction of variables within each type of reorganization and make comparisons. A broad distinction was easily discernible in terms of centripetal and centrifugal forces operating in these families (Farber 1975; Farber 1977). Logically, centripetal forces are more common, for with divorce, most households and families become abbreviated. In their search for help, one portion of the divorcing sample turned to their parents as a source of support, while others maintained the nuclear household as their dominant form of reorganization, albeit in its abbreviated form. In other cases, centrifugal forces were operating, and divorced individuals formed expanded networks of friends and relatives of which parents were only one part. These forms of reorganization were associated with three sets of variables: the type of relationship individuals had with their parents, the composition of their social networks, and their values on the new moralities (Johnson 1988c). This patterning of variables is illustrated in the following types of reorganization.

The Generational Bond

Divorcing parents who reemphasized the bond with their parents shared a cluster of characteristics that distinguished them from others in the sample. At our first contact, these respondents gave their first priority to the solidarity of the intergenerational bond —the blood relationship with their parents and children. The majority who chose this option were women. They were less likely to be dating or cohabiting or to have remarried than were those who chose the other forms of reorganization. These individuals also

Table 3.2

Relationship Emphasis in the Reorganization Process, Time 1
(by percentage)

	Generational (N = 21)	Nuclear (N = 16)	Network (N = 15)
Gender of adult child			
Male	30	35	35
Female	34	41	25
Grandmother's involvement			
Increased contact/child	71	56	21
Increased contact/grandchild	67	31	21
Increased services	90	38	43
Grandmother's services			
Babysitting	76	40	57
Financial help	86	56	43
Intergenerational dependency			
Child on parent	66	38	21
Interdependent	24	6	14
Independent	10	56	57
Grandmother's attitude on child's divorce			
In favor	40	25	14
Reservations	40	31	50
Opposed	20	44	36
Grandmother blames			
Own child	5	13	29
Child-in-law	81	31	7
Neither or both	14	56	64
Personal freedom over family			
Grandmothers	30	33	38
Divorcing children	29	68	60
Approve of cohabitation			
Grandmothers	25	19	46
Divorcing children	44	35	36

were significantly more likely to have economic problems and to be receiving economic help from their parents. They were significantly more dependent on both parents for most of their needs than were others in the sample.

Not surprisingly, most respondents reported a positive relationship with both parents, but they particularly identified their mothers as friends and confidantes. In many cases, respondents described their relationship with their mother as egalitarian and symmetrical, as "best friends" or as "sisters"—perhaps to disguise dependency and the asymmetry it promoted. In fact, in numerous cases, significant economic contributions were disguised as gifts to preserve a feeling of friendship. Divorcing women with such a relationship reported that their mothers influenced their actions. They also had high expectations for their mothers, and on the whole, most of these expectations were met. As one woman explained, "It's an emotionally fragile time in my life. It's great to know Mom is always there." Mothers were occasionally referred to as "my security blanket" or the "ballast in my ship." In several cases, the mother's actions actually prevented young children from being placed in foster homes, which prompted one divorcing daughter to comment, "I owe my mother my soul."

In other cases, mothers and daughters shared the status of divorced women and became close confidantes. "We rehash our divorces all the time and conclude all men are bastards," said one daughter. Closeness usually preceded the dissolution of the marriage. These respondents had used their parents (G1) as confidants during the final stages of their marriage. They were significantly more likely to discuss their problems with their mothers and had found them understanding and supportive. Both their parents were far more likely to have been in favor of the divorce, and, importantly, both they and their parents tended to blame the former spouse for the breakup of the marriage. Not surprisingly, the divorcing individuals had significantly less contact with their in-laws. After divorce, many described their relationship with their former spouse and parents-in-law as hostile.

These divorced parents mainly confined their social activities to family and relatives; they had fewer friends, confidants, or significant others in comparison to others in the sample. With the exception of financial problems, however, they did not vary in the report of the problems they or their children were experiencing. Finally, these respondents also were more traditional in their values; significantly fewer respondents approved of sexual permissiveness, and they were less likely than others in the sample to approve of living together outside of marriage. Both parents and adult children in this group were more likely than others in the sample to agree on their values on family life, giving priority to family interests over egocentric interests. To summarize, these parent—adult child dyads illustrate a traditional relationship that is close and interdependent and one where parents, in the process of extending aid, can exert influence over their children.

The Gordons portray an adaptation to the divorce of their daughter, Ginnie, consistent with this emphasis on the generational bond. The Gordons are in their early sixties, and Mr. Gordon is retired. When their daughter called from the East Coast and said she was coming home with four small children, they immediately mobilized their resources to ease the usual stresses of divorce. They bought a home in their neighborhood so their daughter and grandchildren could live rent-free. When Ginnie Gordon and her children got settled, they and her parents reestablished a very close interdependent tie, a relationship more like they had had in Ginnie's childhood. Mr. Gordon spent his days maintaining both houses and was on call if the children got home from school before their working mother. They were in and out of each others' homes all day. One grandson liked to tag along with his grandfather, and they once took a cross-country camping trip together. If one of the children needed disciplining, Ginnie usually called her father to come over and help as a surrogate father.

Throughout our research, this arrangement worked well. The two households continued to be in daily contact. Since everyone moved easily from one household to the other, they had few secrets from each other. In other words, the boundaries were lowered. Many evenings after the children were in bed, Ginnie left them with her babysitter and went down to her parents' house in her bathrobe. She and her mother would watch television or work on handicrafts. Some evenings they soaked in the hot tub and exchanged the news of the day. Although Ginnie said they disagreed in their political and religious views, she concluded, "I couldn't live without them."

Neither the parents nor their daughter had an active social life outside family contacts. Ginnie was involved in her children's school activities. She went from full-time to part-time work to have more time with her children, and her parents were making up the difference in her income. Ginnie had "no love interest and no interest in remarrying." Most summers they took vacations together along with their son, Ginnie's brother, and his family.

The solidarity between generations created a particularly sharp cleavage with Ginnie's former husband and his family. There was no contact with his parents, who lived in the Midwest, except for telephone calls twice a year. Although her ex-husband remained on the East Coast and had only intermittent contact with his children, that, too, had ended when Mr. Gordon detected "fishy business" during their visits with their father. Apparently his grandson confided having seen explicit sexual scenes while there, so the visitation arrangements were changed. Mrs. Gordon did not work, so most of her leisure time was spent with her children and grandchildren. She and her daughter were closest confidantes. They shared many interests, even favorite television shows. Although the Gordons were making financial sacrifices to help Ginnie and her children, they did not complain. Mr. Gordon insisted, "Even if we are down to our last cent, they are family and we take care of them." This relationship is a good example of how personal interests are suppressed in the interests of preserving the generational bond. Obviously, the grandparents played a key role in minimizing the usual stresses of the divorce process. Possibly their assistance was one reason Ginnie expressed no interest in remarrying. Through their financial help, they also permitted their daughter and grandchildren to maintain a middle-class position. Ginnie provided a well-ordered life for her children, a life that would have been difficult to maintain without her parents' intervention.

The Private, Bounded Nucleated Unit

Divorcing individuals who experienced centripetal forces and attempted to maintain the privacy of their nuclear household made up 31 percent of the sample. In comparison to those who chose solidarity with parents, these divorcing individuals described themselves as relatively isolated from kin, and their relationships with parents and relatives were often summarized as distant. For some respondents, the relationship with their parents was friendly at a distance. Such distance was documented by the report of one grandmother who was friendly with both her son and her daughter-in-law. They all lived in the same suburb, yet she had learned of their separation through friends. Common summaries of this type of parent—adult child relationship were: "We don't go running to each other with every little problem." "We aren't on top of each other all the time." "We bend over backwards not to interfere with each other's lives." As these comments suggest, both parents and their adult children strongly affirmed values on independence, but the divorcing individuals (G2) were more likely than their parents to endorse individualistic interests over family interests (see table 3.2).

Other respondents, in comparison to those who emphasized the generational bond, reported somewhat problematic relationships with their parents. They had significantly less contact with them, and they reported more social distance and conflict in their relationship with their mother. They also reported that their parents had little influence over them and that each generation expected little from the other. We heard such justifications as, "I need space to separate from them." "We are friendly, but I would never confide in them" "My parents are remote—into their own thing."

Their parents had been less informed about the marital problems and tended to take a neutral stance on the processes of marital breakdown.

Respondents in this group were also socially distant from their in-laws. Most described their feelings toward in-laws as neutral—devoid either of warmth or hostility. Although more isolated from kin or in-laws, most had numerous close friends and confidants, and one-half had a lover or a new spouse. There were no significant differences in their reports of problems in comparison to others in the sample, most likely because many of these individuals had a reservoir of friends and lovers as sources of support. Since they also reported fewer economic problems than those dependent on their parents, a major divorce-related stressor was removed. In all, the relationships between parents and adult children in these dyads were ones of distance and reserve, where members of both generations retained their private and independent lives.

The Douglases and their divorced daughter, Susan, are good examples of those who attempt to maintain firm boundaries around their nuclear families even when the divorce has created a vulnerable situation—as it had for Susan and her three preschool children. Susan described her relationship with her parents as superficial. She said she had been independent of them ever since she left home after high school. Then, after the birth of her first child, she "stopped feeling part of their family. My family became my own children, not the family I grew up in." Susan was quite overburdened economically and was trying to work and care for her young children alone. She resented her parents for not trying to help her: "I wanted help and it didn't come. I resent it and I withdraw. But I've never gone to my parents with my hurt feelings and vulnerabilities. They feel confident in my ability to work things out on my own, so I never bring my problems to them."

At our first contact, Susan's life was particularly stressful because she had to both work and care for two young children. Her parents would only take the eldest, concluding the preschoolers were too much for them. By the last contact, the children were four years older, but Susan's financial problems had increased. Her husband had stopped paying child support, so she had had to sell her house and move into a low-income housing project. Her parents did give her some money each month, but it did not make up the difference. Susan concluded her parents were doing about what she expected: "I've never expected much from them. I am not emotionally dependent on them."

Mrs. Douglas confirmed her daughter's judgment that she would rather go out with her many friends than babysit. She also said she was at a new stage in life: she and her husband wanted to travel more and to buy a vacation retreat. She explained: "I need rest. It's time to relax. I feel like a dishrag if I spend any time in Susan's noisy and confusing house. You have to really love her to go see her. I know she gets peeved if I don't help out with babysitting, but I can't help it. She'll work it out. She has been independent from the day she was born. She doesn't communicate with us—the type who clams up. Thank God, she is so capable. She will work it out. We wouldn't rely on her either. My husband and I have each other." Mrs. Douglas confirmed that she retained her active friendship network and didn't feel she had to be responsible for her daughter's well-being: "Susan tries to tell me I should choose my grandchildren over my own life." We help her financially even though we can't afford it. We babysit in a pinch, but usually I'm too tired for that at night. She gets mad, but I say, 'Give me a break.' We do get along, but we clash. Most of the time, I'd prefer to keep my distance." Susan was dating and had an active friendship network. Nevertheless, her financial plight had placed considerable pressure on her and had resulted in some downward mobility. She was seriously considering remarriage.

Loose-knit Social Networks

Also in comparison to those with generational solidarity, those individuals who chose loose-knit networks comprised 35 percent of the families. These individuals tended to favor alternate life-styles over conventional family forms. They reported distant, nonsupportive relationships with their parents and described the relationship as either neutral or, in a few cases, negative. In contrast to all others in the sample, they maintained friendly relationships with in-laws. Their sexual values were permissive, and they placed more emphasis on individualistic over family priorities than did their parents. Their parents, on the other hand, tended to value family priorities.

In such networks, conventional family units were sometimes difficult to identify because their was a blurring between relatives by blood and those by the present marriage and former marriages. In this relatively unbounded, shapeless, and changeable extended family form, adult children usually had friendly but distant relationships with their parents, but they also had friendly relationships with their ex-spouse and former parents-in-law. The majority of respondents were divorced women who had formed coalitions with their former mother-in-law; in the process of receiving help from them, their network of relatives and friends actually became larger. Fewer were dependent upon their parents either emotionally or economically (see table 3.2). Conjugal succession was common among members of these networks; more divorces and remarriages were reported.

One description could apply to many parent–adult child relationships in this group: "We have a mellow relationship. We don't see each other often, but we like each other." Such interactions were based upon personal attraction rather than norms of obligation: "Obligation is an unkind word. We like to be involved because we want to—not because we have to." "We want a distant but loving relationship." Like those with a nucleated focus, independence was stressed. With strong sanctions against interfering with each other's lives, their goal was a fun-loving relationship: "The best thing you can do for a parent is to lead your own life." "I had to reject Mother's influence in order to grow up. Now we have a good relationship." "We don't get upset about anything." "We feel no obligation—both of us do as we please."

In comparison to those with the solidary intergenerational bond, significantly fewer individuals in this group were economically dependent on their parents and fewer reported emotional difficulties. Their mood was less affected by their divorce, and they had a wide range of individuals they could seek out for support if needed. They reported fewer problems with their children, although more of their children had sought professional help than was the case for others in the sample. Both parent and grandparent generations usually maintained friendly relationships with the former spouse and his or her parents and tended to avoid attributing any blame for the divorce. Likewise, individuals in both generations in this family type were more liberal on issues of sexual permissiveness and family values. However, the divorcing individuals differed significantly from their parents in that they gave egocentric interests higher priority than family interests.

The grandparents in these expanded networks also differed from others in the sample (Johnson 1985a; Johnson and Barer 1987). Although grandmothers in general were more conservative in their values than their children were, those who participated in these expanded networks were more flexible in their values on divorce, sexual freedom, and egocentric interests over family interest. In these expanded networks, the grandmothers were more satisfied with their networks, although they found the members less supportive. To summarize this type of relationship, parents and adult children who opted for this form of solidarity maintained a friendly but distant relationship that emphasized sociability over instrumental supports.

Mrs. Albright represents this value orientation. She is in her early sixties and widowed. She recently married an old friend after having lived with him for a year. She has accumulated step and in-law relatives through both her own and her son's marital changes. Her forty-year-old son, David, had ended his own marriage the previous year and was currently living with a woman whom she has never met. He also lost his job as a car salesman and was spending the bulk of his time going to movies and smoking pot. Her attitude was, "He's a big boy now. Those are his problems, so I can just stand back and look on."

Mrs. Albright described her relationship with her son: "We have a mellow relationship. We don't have a lot of contact—he stops by now and then. He doesn't usually ask for money or advice—I think he just wants to see me. I think he is fond of me. We have just about the kind of relationship we should have. He's busy and I'm busy." Although she still maintains a friendship with Barbara, his former wife, she feels no divided loyalties. She can describe the marital failure with objectivity.

I think she had her hands full with David. They had sexual problems—she would tell me all about it. Then they were going into debt while they were waiting for their fortune to come in. Barbara was telephoning me every day. I was her sounding board.

Now I am a friend to David when he comes here. He talks about when he will get his life together at a higher level of consciousness. He sounds so convincing, but when he leaves I feel I've been had. He loves me and would like me to like him even though he blew it.

Mrs. Albright joked about David's lack of a job: "We can't figure out how he does it. We are jealous." She went on, "When he talks of marrying again, I say, 'Do it, fine, do it.' I tell myself I can't wipe his nose forever. I have limited influence. That is why we have such a good relationship." At one point, she did take him in for three months when he had no money. "Can you imagine a son at forty—a pauper. I set a date for him to get out. Paid his first month's rent on an apartment and bought him some clothes for a job interview."

Mrs. Albright was most flexible in her values. In regard to sex, she said, "As long as they close the bedroom door, anything is okay with me." She believed divorce was the best solution to personal unhappiness. She had no difficulty retaining her allegiances to her former daughter-in-law and was pleased that she now lived with a man who was good with the grandchildren. Mrs. Albright's definition of her family included those relatives who lived nearby whom she liked.

Her son describes their relationship as distant but loving. Originally he was critical of his mother for being too distant—"the type you have to make an appointment to see." But now he concludes that she is not judgmental and has loosened up in recent years. "Both parents had a big ego and expected everyone to knock themselves out for them. They were never bankable—regular. Now I don't care about that anymore. I just want to be friends."

Variations in the sample more or less follow the general characteristics outlined in these three examples of family reorganization, so they offer a basis for systematic comparisons. Although many individuals preferred a nuclear family unit, relatively private and distant from parents and relatives, other options became available following divorce and resulted in more supportive social networks. We will see how different types of family organizations following divorce have differing effects on other relatives. All families in the sample shared the same cultural setting and exposure to the same values, although they differed in their endorsement of the values and norms of the subculture. Having prefaced the findings from this research with a consideration of the cultural context and constructed a model that serves to structure the variations among families, we now go on to study how cultural dimensions affect relationships in families and kinship networks.

If family members disagree on these values and on their expectations of each other, they are likely to be ambivalent about family relationships. In such situations, individuals find some mechanism to reduce this ambivalence. One can predict several outcomes. First, where parents and adult children are in agreement on their values, there is undoubtedly less conflict. Nevertheless, the nature of their relationship depends upon whether these values are traditional or modern. If parents and their adult children agree on traditional values, one can assume they have a strong interdepen-

dence. Likewise, if both generations favor the more impulsive behaviors, they permit each other much freedom. If each one protects
the rights and privacy of the nuclear household, then social distance results even when one may need help from the other. And if
the two generations disagree, they are free to distance themselves
from each other.

◇ 4 ◇

THE DIVORCE

FROM a historical perspective, the steep climb in the divorce rate in the early 1960s was merely an accentuation of a long-term increase dating back to the beginning of the United States census in 1867 (Glick and Lin 1986). Although there are few predictions of future trends at this writing, the divorce rate did stabilize at a high level in the early 1980s, at the same time the high remarriage rate began declining. Thus, it is possible that the divorce rate has peaked (Norton and Moorman 1987), although there are no indications of any decline in rates.

Most research on divorce is problem-focused, reporting divorce's adverse effects on parents and children (Hetherington, Cox, and Cox 1982; Longfellow 1979; Wallerstein 1984; Wallerstein and Corbin 1986; Wallerstein and Kelly, 1979). While no attempt will be made here to cite individual reports, most issues of the *Journal of Marriage and the Family* include at least one article on the social and personal problems of divorcing parents and their children. More psychologically oriented perspectives on the process itself see divorce as the culmination of a process of estrangement or a loss of attachment, which is followed by a period of mourning and bereavement. Social science perspectives, in contrast, usually view divorce theoretically as a social process in which one unit of social organization, the family, breaks down and subsequently undergoes reorganization (Cohen 1971). Thus, the process entails transitions for individuals and major changes for the family, changes that encompass not only those events leading up to the separation but also those following the legal end of the marriage.

While numerous problems continue to be associated with divorce, however, this event is increasingly viewed positively as an acceptable means to resolve marital conflict (Ahrons and Rodgers 1987, Levinger 1965). Given the high rates of divorce and remarriage, these marital changes are predictable, not "unscheduled," so they are increasingly referred to as serial monogamy or conjugal succession (Furstenberg and Spanier 1984). Such labels suggest that marital change is now a normative component of the family cycle. As such, marital changes can liberate individuals from unhappy relationships, permitting them the autonomy and freedom to form new, presumably more satisfying, relationships.

Nevertheless, the divorce process is usually a protracted period of social limbo in which there are few guidelines for behavior. As William Goode (1956) has noted, people are not taught how to behave in a socially appropriate manner. In other words, should one act aggrieved or relieved? There are no rules on which relatives one should relate to or who is a relative after divorce. There are no mandates that relatives, even the parents of the divorced individuals, should provide needed supports. In fact, parents have great difficulty in incorporating formerly married children back into their households even when their assistance is sorely needed (Farber 1981). Goode (1956) aptly summarizes this situation by pointing out that our society now permits divorce but does not provide for its consequences. If divorce is an ambiguous situation from a sociological perspective, remarriage is even more so. Andrew Cherlin (1978) describes remarriage as an incomplete institution because there are even fewer norms or guidelines for behavior. Many questions arise: where is home, who is family, how is wealth distributed, and how is the incest taboo extended? Obviously the situation is accentuated for grandparents, leading many to conclude that they must invent the role or reinvent it as the situation changes. This ambiguity is in part due to confusions over their relationship to a former child-in-law. That individual is no longer related to them by marriage but remains the parent of their grandchildren.

LEGAL DEFINITIONS OF MARRIAGE
AND THE FAMILY

Family law tells us much about how a society defines marriage
and the family (Weitzman and Dixon 1980). No-fault divorce has
been in effect in California since 1970. Although this body of laws
has been praised as an enlightened reform, there is concern that the
laws have diminished individuals' personal responsibilities for the
family (Weitzman 1985). No-fault divorce entails the recognition
of "irreconcilable differences" as a cause of marital breakdown.
California has a "pure" no-fault divorce process; that is, it eliminates the adversarial relationship and the notion of interpersonal
justice. It also assumes an absolute equality between husband and
wife, both economically and socially.

Lenore Weitzman (1985) compares new legal conceptions of
marriage and divorce with traditional legal marriage and traditional legal divorce. By definition, marriage is limited to one male
and one female in a monogamous union in which each is expected
to be faithful. Marriage is for the purpose of procreation, and the
family is based upon a division of labor by gender and a hierarchical relationship between husband and wife. When such a marriage
ends, traditional legal divorce requires grounds for divorce, finding
fault, and the sanctioning of the guilty party. Such a divorce also
perpetuates gender-based differences, so males have some responsibility to support females.

Weitzman (1985) concludes that the major shifts in the legal
code are ahead of normative changes, so the parties of divorce
might not always agree with the freedoms granted by law. Traditional divorce rests upon the offense of one party for not living
up to the commitment. The innocence or guilt of one partner
must be determined, for the injured party has the right to remain
married. Since the party at fault faces economic sanctions, there
is a disincentive for violating the commitment and seeking
divorce. In contrast, the new legal no-fault divorce offers no
such disincentive; it eliminates the adversary relationship and in

doing so eliminates the doctrine of personal responsibility. In Weitzman's opinion (1985), the new freedoms permitted in our changing legal codes are placing women and children in more vulnerable situations.

The level of the father's responsibility for his children may be less stable under no-fault divorce. Such an outcome was observed in this research. For example, with the equitable division of assets, the family home usually needed to be sold at a specified time and the profits divided evenly. In some cases, mother and children were forced to leave a middle-class neighborhood and find low-income housing. In other cases, men's economic responsibility to children ended with their eighteenth birthday, so college-bound children were not able to continue their education. In fact, a ten-year study of children of divorce confirms our impressions; even well-to-do fathers withdraw financial support to children at age eighteen (Wallerstein and Corbin 1986). Since divorced women in this sample and in most studies have significantly less income than divorced men, the assets they received in the settlement were often used for daily expenses. Very few men paid a level of child support sufficient to meet the high cost of living in these suburbs. Without well-defined paternal responsibility, fathers often withdrew or were perceived by their children to be more distant and unavailable to them (Johnson, Schmidt, and Klee, 1988).

STAGES IN THE DIVORCE PROCESS

In their analysis of the divorce process, researchers usually identify several stages through which individuals pass (Ahrons 1980; Levinger 1979; and Newcomb and Bentler 1981). First, individuals in a failing marriage experience a period of marital conflict and personal unhappiness when the idea of divorce comes to mind. Frequently they seek outside help in an effort to save the marriage. Second comes the process of marital dissolution when one partner leaves the household. After varying lengths of time, the divorce itself occurs, and the end of the marriage is legally recognized. The formal determinations of custody of minor children and division of property are made. The third stage, the post-divorce period, is a period of adaptation to a new status. In many cases, this stage entails the formation of new liaisons and reconstituted families. This process is usually dynamic, with changes taking place at a fast pace. At each stage, individual actions are influenced by a host of psychological and social factors. Because much freedom is granted to the individual to make personal choices, these actions are also quite varied.

An analysis of divorce as a series of stages shows that individuals make decisions based upon three types of criteria (Levinger 1965). First, they evaluate the attractions the relationship holds for them and the material, emotional, and symbolic rewards a spouse provides. If these attractions decline, conflicts arise. At this stage, individuals frequently call in various types of professionals or they join self-help groups to help them deal with their failing marriage. In the therapeutic process, individuals examine their motivations and seek solutions, which determine the ultimate outcome of the relationship. Second, individuals evaluate the costs and rewards a divorce would entail. The costs impose some barriers to divorce; individuals may evaluate their personal responsibilities to their children and any social and economic sanctions that may result. Third, when the justifications for the divorce mount and overshadow the barriers to divorce, individuals may seek new relationships that are more attractive to them than their marriage; these new relationships influence the decisions they ultimately make (Levinger 1965).

Several factors operate today to facilitate the use of divorce as a means to resolve marital conflict. For one thing, marital relationships can be sorely tested because individuals have excessive expectations of a spouse. Such a situation creates a psychologically intense relationship, which in itself may be a source of conflict. In the eyes of many individuals, a couple should not only fulfill each other's social and economic needs but also should take the primary responsibility for each other's emotional well-being. If a spouse has the responsibility to make one happy, then he or she is likely to fail to meet such expectations.

When marital conflicts occur in communities where the barriers to divorce are rapidly declining, they can take on more serious implications. Unlike the past, when more traditional economic, social, and moral sanctions were in place to discourage divorce, two individuals make decisions that determine the stability of their marriage with relatively little outside pressure. The absence of social pressures undoubtedly accounts for the increased incidence of divorce. In areas with a high divorce rate, such as at the site of this research, a large pool of eligible mates is available, which further decreases the attractions of the marriage. With these major changes in the social organization of the family, the ensuing process of reorganization entails changes not only in individuals (Weiss 1979) but also in three types of social phenomena: the household, family roles, and dyadic relationships between two individuals. At each stage in the process, then, divorce affects not only individuals in the nuclear family but also members of the kinship system.

Finding Causes of Divorce

Although our major interests were in intergenerational relationships, discussions with both divorced individuals and their mothers were often dominated by long descriptions of the stressful events of separation and divorce. Divorcing respondents related to us a marital history of changing expectations, personal unhappiness, and complaints of unmet needs. The respondents often searched for distractions from their unhappy situation—work, self-actualization therapies, or extramarital affairs. Such searches, however, appeared to be more a symptom of a failing marriage than an objective cause for divorce. At some point, the decision was made to separate, an event commonly referred to as "splitting"—"I was miserable and I split."

It is quite difficult to pinpoint objective causes of divorce in this sample. Demographic evidence indicates that divorce is more common at lower socioeconomic levels (Glenn and Supanic 1984). Since socioeconomic status was controlled in this sample, one important variable associated with divorce was removed. Also, since all of these divorcing respondents had a parent in the area, the problem of social integration, also associated with high divorce rates, was not generally evident. There were few reports of other causes of divorce, such as substance abuse or infidelity. Both parents and adult children reported far less explicit reasons for divorce. The vague causes reported ranged from moralistic judgments on social decay to subtle problems in relationships. One must agree with William Goode (1956), who points out that any serious student of divorce must drop the search for causes. Marital failure cannot be traced to a single factor, for causes can be attributed to a partner's behavior, to problems in the relationship, or to broader social factors.

Respondents in both generations often pointed to a value system that has made divorce more acceptable. The grandparents frequently placed the blame on the "me" generation, a generation of individuals who put their own interests above their families. They condemned the courses and books that "teach people to be self-centered." Since the divorcing generation so widely endorsed their right to personal happiness, however, any condemnations usually fell on deaf ears.

In the belief system of the divorcing generation, a spouse should make one happy. The failure to do so was often viewed as justifiable grounds for divorce. At some point, individuals re-evaluated their marriage and their commitments to a spouse. As one respondent noted, her former husband was virtually faultless in all areas except "the ability to take care of my psyche." With this individual and many others, high expectations for emotional succor resulted in a marital relationship in which these expectations could not be met. Subsequently, individuals were likely to find more attractive alternatives to their marriage (Cuber and Haroff 1965; Goode 1959).

Many respondents complained of personal unhappiness, which they traced to their marriages. We concluded that it was impossible to sort out whether the symptoms of unhappiness were associated with a problematic marriage or with other sources. Moreover, errant behaviors of a spouse may or may not have been a manifest cause of divorce. Simple answers are less easily found today, particularly in states such as California where no-fault divorce legally justifies divorce on the basis of irreconcilable differences. Without the legal necessity to find cause, researchers have a difficult task eliciting simple answers from respondents.

In setting up coding categories, we arrived at around thirteen "causes" reported by the respondents. These ranged from clear-cut justifications, such as abandonment or "becoming gay," to rather fuzzy references to personality differences, poor communication, or simply the need to find a happier situation. Although the sample size is too small to make generalizations, the most frequent "causes" suggest the dominant concerns of the respondents. The most commonly mentioned causes of divorce were psychological in nature. Personality differences led to flaws in the relationship. In their search for a happier situation, they turned to divorce as a solution. Communication problems were also commonly reported, so psychological problems evidently were difficult to resolve. Together these vague reasons constituted over 40 percent of all causes mentioned by the divorcing individuals.

In their pursuit of a happier situation, some respondents had affairs. It was common for both husbands and wives to report occasional affairs throughout the marriage. While both might have been tolerant of each other's behavior, at some point this tolerance ended and the marriage was affected. Misunderstandings developed that led to the breakup of the marriage. One respondent commented, "Without discussing it, we both assumed we had an open marriage—that we were free to have affairs as long as it didn't get out of hand."

Sexual problems were commonly reported. These reports ranged from vague references to sexual difficulties to a change in sexual orientation. The important point here is that, except for a minority of the divorces, we could identify few objective causes of divorce. For example, only 9 percent mentioned financial difficulties and 7 percent mentioned drug or alcohol abuse. Somewhat surprisingly, only a few individuals initiated divorce because they were in love with another. Thus, few individuals left a marriage with the immediate intention of remarrying. In fact, many voiced the resolution to take one's time in making such a decision. Some even resolved never to marry again, usually because they enjoyed the prospect of being free of commitments for the first time in their lives.

The "search for happiness" was so frequently mentioned that one can tentatively suggest that it is a major criterion for evaluating marital success. We also frequently heard the theme that time was running out, that to find happiness one had to make a move before becoming too old. "I'd been miserable for years. At a point that a close friend died, I decided that life is too short—it was time to split." Others looked to the future with dread: "I couldn't imagine spending the next thirty years with her. I deserve a happier life." Finally, as one man reported, "I realized it was time to either fish or cut bait."

Efforts to Save the Marriage

The importance attached to personal happiness appears to be reinforced by many therapists in the area. At the time we interviewed them, almost half of the respondents were still receiving professional help. Various therapeutic techniques flourish in these suburbs. They range from conventional psychotherapy and psychoanalysis to est, encounter groups, or consciousness groups.

These therapies focus specifically on the individual and his or her problems in adapting. They often explicitly place a priority on self-realization or self-actualization as the basis for personal happiness and family success. For example, respondents often reported their therapists telling them their children's problems could only be alleviated when they solved their own problems. Or "He tells me I have to think of myself."

When a marriage was in trouble, couples frequently went into "counseling," a term that they explicitly distinguished from therapy. Counseling addressed problems in the relationship and was sought as a means either to reorganize the marriage or to ease the strains of divorce. In many cases, counseling appeared to function far more successfully in the divorce process than it functioned to preserve the marriage. "We had a lousy marriage, but we really have a compatible divorce" was one description of the beneficial effects of counseling. Counseling also eased the strains of transition to a new status. It was initiated near the end of the marriage, and before the formal mediation required by law in California. When all hopes of reconciliation were abandoned, mediation addressed the division of property and the determination of custody.

In the counseling process itself, it was not uncommon for divorcing individuals to meet new individuals, who became formidable competition to a spouse. Individuals who used these therapies were less prone to assign blame to a former partner, so this form of help was in some measure successful. It helped them avoid excessive conflict during the stressful post-divorce period. In fact, only around half of the divorced respondents blamed their former spouse, while some blamed themselves or blamed "neither one" or "both of us." These attributions implied that the separation was unavoidable, an event that simply happened and to which no cause could be assigned.

The wives were significantly more likely to initiate the separation—56 percent in comparison to 25 percent of the husbands who were initiators. In the remaining 19 percent, a mutual agreement was made to separate. By the time we interviewed these individuals, an average of twenty-four months after the separation, 65 percent of the husbands and 78 percent of the wives viewed the divorce as a good solution. This does not mean, however, that they found the process easy. Many pointed to long periods of stress, conflict, depression, and, most frequently, loneliness.

Lowering the Barriers to Divorce

Divorcing individuals consisted roughly of two age groups—those under thirty-five years old, who had small children and middle-aged parents, and individuals divorcing in middle age, who had parents in old age. The younger divorcing parents, on the whole, grew up in relatively privileged families in Northern California middle-class suburbs, where the self-actualization movement has flourished for some years. Based on interviews with their mothers, one can conclude that these younger divorcing individuals were usually raised permissively and encouraged to pursue personal growth and fulfillment. As adolescents they were familiar with or participated in the many social movements in the 1960s. It was not uncommon to hear of moves to the Haight Ashbury area of San Francisco or becoming flower children or part of the drug revolution. Despite their high-class backgrounds, half of the divorcing generation did not finish college. In some cases, they quit school and traveled around the world or lived in communes. In other words, many lived out the experiences of the sixties. Numerous couples lived together for some time, only marrying when there was a pregnancy.

The older divorcing men and women were usually more established in conventional middle-class suburban life, but from time to time they could adopt the stances and even the life-styles of their younger counterparts. They, too, were not immune to the new values and life-styles of the area. In fact, jokes are made about the stereotype of the middle-aged divorced man who buys a BMW, wears gold chains on his hairy chest exposed by an unbuttoned shirt, and joins a health club to trim his waistline.

The barriers to divorce also appear to have been weak with the grandparent generation. One-quarter of the divorcing individuals had divorced parents, a relatively high percentage for the generations now in late middle age or old age. At the end of the study, 38 percent had divorced siblings. Thus, patterns of marital instability had been fairly well established for some time, and given the permissiveness of the environment, the barriers to divorce were weak. In a broad view, in such a social setting, a high divorce rate was likely (Glenn and Supanic 1984). The rapid social changes taking place here had liberated many individuals from pressures to conform to conventional family values. As noted above, formal professional or paraprofessional therapies as well as the lay movements in the area offered therapeutic supports that often strengthened intentions to form new lives free from traditional ties. Even many churches devoted their efforts to easing the strains of divorce rather than preserving the marriage. Thus, another major barrier to divorce was removed.

The children of divorce rarely suffered the stigma of having divorced parents. In fact, divorce was so common in this area that even elementary schools had counseling or group therapy for young children. Teachers were particularly attentive to custody arrangements, so that report cards and school announcements reached the appropriate parent. To illustrate the general norm, it was reported that one ten-year-old boy who had recently moved to the area had great difficulty in adjusting. His complaint centered on his envy of other children, who were very involved in their large expanded families consisting not only of parents, grandparents, and siblings, but also of stepparents, stepgrandparents, and stepsiblings. He was also continually frustrated by attempts to locate other children as they shifted from house to house of parents and even grandparents.

In settings such as the one studied here, where there are few normative sanctions against divorce and where there are more divorces each year than marriages, divorce is an option one can take without sanctions. Also, when families have adequate resources, divorce does not always impose the formidable barrier of financial hardship.

Alternative Attractions

Given the numbers of age peers who were also divorced, the dating process usually started soon after the separation. Not surprisingly, two-thirds of the sample were dating at our first contact. To mention a few examples, one woman began dating and eventually married the marriage counselor she and her husband had sought when their marriage was failing. Another woman began going out with the lawyer who had arranged her divorce. Another had an affair with the carpenter who was renovating her house. Other men and women commiserated with old friends about their divorces, and in the process, new relationships formed. One woman explained: "He often stopped by to chat about getting resettled. I was going through the same thing, so we understood each other. Then we became more serious."

Because of the open situation, rearrangements in marital status affected a series of marriages. In one case, a divorced middle-aged woman felt abandoned by her former husband. She described the period as the most miserable in her life. Then an old high school sweetheart appeared on the scene. After spending a few months renewing their old bond, he decided to divorce his wife and marry her. Being married does not necessarily deter affairs from developing, and some go on for years if a divorce and property settlement is too costly. For example, a divorced woman with two children began an affair with a married man soon after her separation. He refused to divorce his wife for religious reasons, but that stance did not interfere with their relationship. For the four years we followed this sample, he spent every Friday night with her. He was even included in her family gatherings, which in this case included not only her own family but also her former husband's parents. In all, the large pool of eligibles offers attractive alternatives, which may initially hasten the end of some marriages. Since there are few sanctions against forming liaisons, these attractions are even further facilitated. That numerous respondents referred to their divorce as a growth experience suggests the appeal of new relationships.

PATHWAYS TO DIVORCE

Analysis of the data showed there were three types of divorce processes, each entailing differing levels of involvement of the older generation. First and most commonly, both husband and wife mutually agreed upon the divorce through rational decision-making processes. Often both partners timed the divorce to their convenience and to a predetermined time when they felt the stress to children would be minimized. In such cases, the grandparents were rarely involved except as remote observers.

Second, in other cases, the divorce occurred in the heat of emotions after much bitterness and acrimony. Often this bitterness occurred in the midst of bouts of alcohol or drug abuse. In several other cases, one partner ran away, abandoning not only a spouse but also young children. When young children were involved, the grandparents often played an important role, even to the point of becoming surrogate parents to the grandchildren. If their relationship with their child had previously been close and interdependent, grandparents also became their child's confidants and defenders.

Third, it was not uncommon for a couple to dissolve the marriage without either intentional plans or conflict and bitterness. This pattern occurred most often in open marriages, in which extramarital affairs were acceptable to both partners. There was implicit agreement that each one had some sexual freedom as long as they preserved some measure of propriety and did not overstep the implicit boundaries by becoming too emotionally involved with a lover. Generally, those who espoused open marriage held few resentments later toward an ex-spouse. The divorce was viewed as an acceptable means of resolving marital conflict, and remarriage was taken for granted. These were the individuals who were likely to form amorphous kinship networks.

In approximately one-third of the sample, the divorce was described as friendly: "We are mutually loving and supportive." "We've remained good friends—I still love him." In 25 percent of the cases, as illustrated below, a neutral relationship was retained: "We're civil, but there's little to say." "We avoid confrontation. We only talk about the children." "We get along—there's no conflict any more." "No change from the marriage—there's no hate, but no love either." In the remainder, 42 percent, much hostility remained, usually at a distance: "We arrange it so we never have to meet. If we met, we'd fight all the time."

Grandparents were rarely informed about the extramarital affairs. In fact, only one-third of the grandparents were involved in the actual decision-making processes that led to divorce. Even where they were in frequent contact and functioned as confidants to their children, they were not well informed on the intimate details of the marriage. Observant grandparents on occasion noted signs of marital unhappiness, but by and large they were inactive at this stage. Children often felt unable to discuss their problems with a parent, either because they did not want to worry them or because they felt they would not understand. Grandparents, then, were not actively involved in the processes of marital breakdown, and in only a few cases were they a source of conflict in the marriage. Most were sympathetic and concerned observers at a distance at this stage in the process. Thus, there were few proverbial troublesome and interfering mothers-in-law in this sample. As long as their child's marriage was intact, and in keeping with the strong beliefs on the privacy and independence of the nuclear household, these women maintained their distance. Only with the departure of the child-in-law did they permit themselves to take needed actions.

A Divorce After Long-Term Deliberation

Those who divorced by mutual agreement often remained on friendly terms, a situation that often extended to each other's new spouses. In some cases, the formerly married and their reconstituted families celebrated holidays together and amiably planned jointly for graduation parties or other ritual occasions of their children. In several instances, they even attended each other's weddings. One example of a nonconflictual divorce process was reported by Julie, a thirty-six-year-old mother of two children. She was still living in the family home, a modest dwelling in a suburban tract. Her father had retired, and her parents traveled constantly in their mobile home. Thus, they were not in frequent contact with Julie and her children. Her former husband's parents lived on the East Coast and rarely visited. Julie began immediately to describe her separation and divorce.

My idea is don't drag out the separation. It only makes people miserable. We talked about it for a year. We tiptoed around it. There was no way I'd move out of this house. I am here to stay. It just took him some time to figure it out. Our marriage had been dying for five years. It is hard to stay in an insidious situation. It made me sick to have this man floating around the house.

It was a traditional marriage. I felt like a paperdoll, a kept woman. He was traditional, wanting to dole out money like I was a child. It made me feel that I had no control over my life. The only thing we shared was anger and ice—a very icy relationship. It was pretty insidious, but under the surface. He never beat me or drank. I just have to say that we broke up because we didn't get along.

We were also like two children not being able to get what we wanted. We both felt insignificant and worthless. If I saw his socks left out, I got mad instead of saying it's not his fault. There was a lot of anger and frustration, which created a big gulf between us.

Sex was really crummy with us. That was the worst part of our marriage. All of our problems were expressed in our sex life. Earlier, I had told him, you can stay, but I can't have sex with you any more. I can't have sex with a man I don't like. So our relationship ended. It was bad for someone to make it last that long. I felt so worthless. I felt that I was in collusion with something bad.

I went to a counselor about this lousy situation. He said that I have to think of myself first. He felt I'd be a lousy parent if I didn't get out of this morass. And he helped me overcome doubt and a sense of failure.

In commenting on the actual event of separation, she described
their reasoned actions.

> A week before he moved out, he told me he had rented an apart-
> ment in the city. I was surprised—I never thought he would make
> the move. I said, "Fine. We'll tell the children on Saturday." He
> was surprised I agreed so easily.
>
> When he told the children, there was the shock and tears at
> first, but then they went on eating their cereal, and the discussion
> was over. We decided what time their daddy should go to his new
> apartment, and we all helped him pack. Then we drove in two cars
> into the city and helped him unpack at his bachelor's pad. I took
> my camera along and took a picture of the children sitting with
> their father on the couch in his new place. After unloading his
> stuff, we all went out for lunch. When the children and I started
> back home, we stopped and I took their picture on the bridge just
> to let them know that that was where they really belong.
>
> My only qualms came when I pulled back into the driveway
> here. I thought, Jesus, what have I done? I am alone—I may be
> alone forever. The emptiness, the feeling of not having any feet. For
> the first time in my life, I was alone. I had no one. God damn, it
> is hard. I really am not a strong, responsible person—the never-
> ending responsibility. If you have to be disciplinarian and a parent
> too, it's an enormous responsibility. The finances had to be worked
> out. The house was falling apart. But my life is still better.

As in many cases of marital discord, the relationship between
husband and wife improved after the divorce.

> Now there is an absence of conflict. And sometimes I ask him
> what he's doing, and he's friendly too. The first time he asked me
> about my love life and sexual activity, I was shocked. We were
> having lunch after signing the formal decree—or was it when we
> were closing our joint checking account? I was holding a margarita.
> With the shock, my hand shook so much the drink splattered onto
> my food.

An Acrimonious Divorce

Divorces that were conflictual most often involved antisocial behavior of one or both partners—excessive intake of alcohol or recreational drugs. If young children were involved, the grandparents usually played a critical role, acting as stabilizers in the midst of the ensuing social disorganization. For example, Cindy, a thirty-five-year-old mother of two children, ages two and four, had married Kevin only because she was pregnant. Through four stormy years they stayed together. They both came from upper-middle-class professional backgrounds, but had opted for a life on the fringes between a hippie community and the suburb in which she had been raised. They were intermittently employed in unskilled jobs, and their lives were punctuated by frequent intake of alcohol and drugs.

Both had decided that with the birth of their children they would settle down into more conventional family life. The responsibilities of parenthood, however, appeared to be too much for both of them. Kevin worked irregularly, and he refused to pay bills even though the power company had threatened to turn off their electricity. When pressures mounted, Cindy turned to drugs, and on several occasions, she disappeared for several days. She described this period as "when I had my nervous breakdown. I was much more out of it than I let on to my parents. God, I needed someone to tell me, 'Get your shit together.' Kevin lost interest in me when I had children. He was always spaced-out and was violent at times. It was like a nightmare. I was always on the phone to Mother—so much so that she was getting sick of it. She finally told me, 'Either you leave him, move in here, and enter a detox program or else don't tell me another word about it.'" Cindy's mother confirmed these events.

I was terrified for her—that she would hurt herself and the children. The drugs and running off were out of character for her.

It was very self-destructive. I knew she was desperate. Every Sunday they would be here for dinner. It was a normal family setting. Then, during the week, all hell would break loose. It was a horrible mess—each week it was repeated. She would tell me all her trials and tribulations. At first I said, "You're married to him. It's up to you to figure it out." But deep down I knew it would never work out. He's like a nonperson—has no sense of responsibility. He wears old clothes. Now he has no home of his own—just finds someone and moves in with them. He seems to get away with it. He doesn't file income tax, no bank account. It's funny though, I think he wanted to marry and have a family life—he just didn't know how to go about it.

I'm glad it's all over—it was like a nightmare. I'm glad we were here and could help. All through her life, she has known she has this place to come to. She only stayed a year, but that was long enough to get things straightened out.

Cindy concluded her discussion by telling us: "I owe my parents my soul. If it hadn't been for them, terrible things might have happened. As it was, I could whisk my children out of a bad situation and start a new life."

Unintentional Marital Breakdown

Perhaps one of the best ways to illustrate the many dimensions of divorce is to describe a divorce in which causes were elusive. In the following example, the divorce of Bill and Alice Franklin appears to have occurred despite their best intentions to work out their problems. They both described a progressive alienation from each other. A series of affairs took place at the time Bill was finishing his medical training and setting up his practice. Alice finally initiated the separation after several years of conflict and two trial separations. She moved in with another man after having a brief affair with him.

Bill and Alice were childhood sweethearts and married during college. The parents of both partners had maintained friendly relationships with each other and with their former child-in-law. Both sets of parents had been very pleased with the marriage and were quite upset when it ended. All concluded that there was no reason their relationship should end. In fact, they had all made attempts at mediation; but when their efforts were rebuffed, all four parents stayed tactfully at a distance and strove to avoid interfering with the events taking place.

Bill was interviewed in his office one late afternoon. In responding to our questions on how his parents learned of the divorce, he explained:

> I first discussed it with my father. I told him things were screwed up. I didn't want to talk to my mother because she takes things emotionally and personally. I didn't want her involved in my life in her hype emotional way. I figured my dad was more available in an emotional way. Though recently I've had some good conversations with my mother. She is an all-inclusive person, which makes it hard. She doesn't understand the limits of the family.
>
> When Alice left, I flipped out. I was so angry. She was away for six weeks—just before I had to take my boards. I broke down. I thought of killing myself. I was mad at my wife. My anger, though, kept depression at bay. I had to study. I led a monastic life. She came back after my boards, but I got badly depressed. Only later did I focus on getting things together. We saw a marriage counselor. But I pulled out of it when she started getting her things out of the house. Now I'm trying to get all the memories of my ex-wife out of my life.
>
> It had made sense to get married. But it didn't fit my rational plan because I had to finish medical school and residency and set my direction. Before settling down, I wanted a good sense of self first.
>
> She wouldn't communicate—she'd turn over and go to sleep when problems needed discussing. She brought nothing to the marriage. She just took over my interests—it didn't expand my life.

While Bill was in training, they spent three years in the Northeast—a period when additional strains were placed on the relationship. Bill described that period:

> The isolation from our families made our relationship more important. Then I finally realized the relationship was in trouble— we were distant and she felt threatened. I felt like dating other women even though she was pregnant. She was not relating to me positively. For a while after the baby was born, things changed a lot. The baby was so exciting that first year. Our marriage was only about having a kid.
>
> Then, when we came back to California, things came loose. I moved Alice and the baby back to live with her parents, and I went back to finish the last few months of training. I had a great time alone. I was doing my own thing and it felt fantastic. I had a girl friend. At that time Alice was having problems making adjustments here. I couldn't tolerate her inability to do things. Things just fell apart. I felt trapped. My relationships were diversions. Alice also had a relationship with a man that was at odds with our marriage. She was emotionally unavailable to me.
>
> Lots of factors were involved. Neither of us were supportive to the other. Immaturity had a lot to do with it. It was hard for me to have a kid and be in training. It was complex. My achievements and her stagnation pointed each other up. It was a vicious circle. Eventually we both looked outside the marriage for meaningful relationships.
>
> We drifted apart, but she is the one who split. I felt abandoned. My focus had been to try to make it work. I'm over the agony of it. Now I feel the need to live with someone else, but she is not the one.

Alice described these same events:

> We were living in the gray, dreary Northeast. It was sorta the beginning of things not going the way I wanted them to. At that time, I thought I'd have the baby, put her in a backpack, and life would be unchanged; but it didn't work out that way. I was house-

bound. I had no friends. The gray climate was getting to me. I was giving up my career in art.

When we came back here, Bill was still in training. I worked as a waitress and had other odd jobs. I still don't know what happened to our marriage. The problem was—we were living too close to our parents. We never grew up. It was getting claustrophobic.

After a year, I was back in art school. I met a man who I soon became involved with for at least a year. My husband knew about it and hated me for it. It led to my moving out for a month. We hadn't agreed to have an open marriage—it was completely off the wall. In the East, we both had brief little affairs, which we told each other about. It balanced out, but it seemed to set the tone, though, for then he had a long involvement with a colleague.

All this time, over two years, we were growing apart. We continued seeing other people. Then I started an affair with one of Bill's good friends. He got really angry with me—you know, the double standard thing. Then I had an opportunity to housesit—it was a good excuse to split. We both hoped, though, that over the summer being apart would make a difference, but it didn't.

We separated a year and a half ago. We tried counselors, but talking we were never good at. Seven or eight months ago, I decided I would go back to him. But he's the one who said forget it. It switched around. Before Bill had wanted to get back together. When I said I wanted to come back, he said he wasn't interested anymore.

In this case, causes are impossible to sort out; immaturity, psychological problems, infidelity, and any number of reasons would apply. Nevertheless, an analysis of the whole process suggests that the divorce was not intentional, that a stage-by-stage alienation led to declining commitments to the marriage. The informal efforts of the parents were ineffective in stemming the events taking place. Liaisons with others added further distance to the relationship, a distance that made reconciliation impossible. Since there were numerous alternative sources of attraction, the individuals easily found substitutes for their spouse.

The point to be made here is that without barriers to divorce or even to extramarital liaisons, events can outpace intentions. Without sanctions against having affairs, without norms that discourage divorce, and without a sense of responsibility to the other person, the individual has great personal freedom. Such freedom can lead, as it did above, to actions that are either later regretted or not well understood.

Perhaps this situation is best illustrated by the remarks of one divorced woman at our second interview, four years after her separation.

> I haven't the vaguest idea why I divorced. I said to a friend the other day that I don't know how I felt when I knew I wanted to end my marriage. I know I was angry and frustrated. I can conjure up those feelings. But I don't know why I ended the marriage. And it is rather crucial. My anger didn't add up to leaving the marriage. I guess you don't need reasons if the feelings are wrong. But is it enough? I wish I could say he was an alcoholic or ran around with women.

DIVORCE'S AFTERMATH

At the point in the process when we interviewed these divorcing individuals—less than three years after the separation and an average of nine months after the divorce—the needs of both men and women still remained high. The most pressing needs that were not being met were the financial ones; 34 percent of the women and 20 percent of the men reported economic difficulties. Over a third of the men and women reported that their psychological needs were not being met. About 15 to 20 percent of the women needed more childcare or household services.

The proportion needing help undoubtedly would have been much larger if these individuals had been less competent in enlisting the supports of an active social network. They had numerous sources of support and were quite skillful in mobilizing family, friends, and professionals to their cause. About an equal proportion of men and women, two-thirds in all, were receiving help from their parents, mainly instrumental help such as money and child-care. An even larger proportion, 88 percent, had friends from whom they could seek emotional help. Almost half were receiving help of some kind from professionals or paraprofessionals—counselors, psychotherapists, clergy, or self-help groups. About 30 percent were able to turn to their children for help, and almost one-quarter of the women were receiving help from their former parents-in-law. Finally, 70 percent of the men and 47 percent of the women had lovers who assisted them in adapting to the post-divorce period. Women were at a greater disadvantage economically; only 14 percent had monthly incomes of over two thousand dollars, while 54 percent of the men did.

While only a few couples continued to share social activities, a large majority was able to avoid conflict. Men, on the whole, were involved with their children. In 7 percent of the divorces, custody was granted to the father, and in 20 percent, custody was joint. There is some discrepancy between reports of fathers' involvement with childcare. Although 48 percent of the women interviewed reported that their former husbands were not involved in childcare, 80 percent of the men reported they were active to the extent of having at least weekly contact with children. In most cases, women were the significant parents following divorce, irrespective of the father's involvement.

In regard to stress-related symptoms, 29 percent of the respondents reported health problems and 79 percent discussed some psychological problems. Despite these problems, however, 71 percent reported that their morale had improved since their divorce. Over half of them told us that their social activities had increased since their divorce, a predictable finding given their active social networks.

Overall, the divorce had some impact on their children; 59 percent of the parents felt that at least one child in their family had been negatively affected, and 31 percent of the children were receiving professional help. At least one child in a family had divorce-related problems: 62 percent were affected in their overall mood; one-half had problems in school; and 44 percent had some kind of behavioral problem. Frequently, parents and grandparents singled out one child in a sibling group who was particularly affected by the divorce. In any case, respondents often attributed the children's problems to sources other than the divorce itself. Perhaps the relatively low incidence of problems reported among the children in the divorcing families can be traced to the presence of grandparents and their responses to the needs of their children and grandchildren.

◇ 5 ◇

GRANDPARENTING IN DIVORCING FAMILIES

WITH the large numbers of children currently affected by divorce, grandparents constitute a potential family resource to provide support and comfort. Until recently, however, there had been little systematic research on the grandparent role, so there was no clear understanding of their capacities in such situations (Wilson and Deshane 1982). Practitioners working with the family nevertheless have pointed an accusatory finger at grandparents for failing in their family responsibilities (Kornhaber and Woodward 1981). One noted childrearing expert has published a book, *How to Grandparent* (Dodson 1981), which addresses every conceivable problem grandparents might face. Chapters range from "How to Talk to Grandchildren" to "How to Sensitize Yourself to Problem Situations." While not hesitant to give advice in other areas, Dodson was notably vague in his chapter on divorce. He advised grandparents to avoid being a parent figure out of a sense of obligation and to respond only if they felt like helping their grandchildren.

In the scholarly literature, the statistical patterns of grandparenting have been described as ones of diversity rather than of central tendency (Troll 1980), a conclusion that can apply to the wide variations in this sample. Objective variables such as the ages of grandmothers and grandchildren explain some of this diversity. After such variables are accounted for, other sources of variation are more difficult to pinpoint. For example, diversity is often traced to the vagueness of the norms that regulate the role (Bengtson 1985; Troll 1980). It is also possible, however, that grandparenting is not so much a result of normlessness as it is a response to the characteristics of the American family (Apple 1956; Sprey and Matthews 1982). For example, norms of noninterference may prevent grandparents from taking the initiative. As the following indicates, grandparenting also varies according to the type of relationship they have with their children and children-in-law.

The differing views on grandparenting have led to attempts to depict the role in terms of styles—the "funseeker," the "formal," the "distant," or the "parent surrogate" grandmother (Neugarten and Weinstein 1964; Robertson 1977). Their search for style may reflect the lack of content these researchers have found in the role. For example, life satisfaction is not associated with how one grandparents (Wood and Robertson 1978), and grandchildren are not usually a source of support for older people. In fact, a common saying among grandparents is, When in need, one good friend is more important than a dozen grandchildren (Blau 1973). Apparently the symbolic meaning of grandparenthood is more significant than their actions (Kivnick 1982).

In their review of the literature, Kahana and Kahana (1970) point out that the grandparent role has a ritualized quality and is often a "state of mind" rather than a functioning role. Most grandparents reject the authority and nurturing functions of parenting, so the substantive content of the role is notably thin (Neugarten and Weinstein 1964). Since the role of grandparent also is likely to be based upon personal qualities and preferences rather than normative directives, it is an achieved rather than an ascribed role.

The extent to which the role of a grandparent changes with the divorces and remarriages of children has not been widely studied. In the Cherlin and Furstenburg research (1986), the grandchildren were teenagers and the divorce had occurred more than seven years prior to their study. Cherlin and Furstenberg found that maternal grandmothers had more contact with grandchildren than did paternal grandmothers. In one of the few reports of kinship relationships following divorce, Spicer and Hampe (1975) found that high levels of interaction were maintained with consanguineal relatives and that there was a decrease in contact with relatives of a former marriage. Maternal grandparents usually were more active after a divorce, although there was some evidence that a custodial mother was likely to retain relationships with her former in-laws (Anspach 1976; Johnson and Barer 1987; Sprey and Matthews 1982). In a reverse flow of reciprocity, divorce also appears to diminish the capacity of children to provide supports to older parents (Cicirelli 1983b).

TWO GRANDPARENTING STYLES

Before describing the responses of this sample of grandmothers, it is useful to illustrate with two case studies the range of responses grandmothers have to changes in the lives of their children and grandchildren. We can then indicate variables associated with these responses. First, Mrs. Earlham is a flamboyant, youthful-looking woman in her late fifties who has married and divorced several times. She had always been actively involved in her daughter's married life and in fact spent most weekends helping her daughter and her grandchildren. After her daughter's divorce, she learned with dismay that her former son-in-law considered her as too involved and one source of problems in the marriage. Nevertheless, Mrs. Earlham attempted to maintain a friendly relationship with him, so there was no impediment to her continued activity with her grandchildren. Each Friday she picked up her grandchildren, a girl and a boy, ten and twelve years of age, and brought them to her house for the night. Each Saturday morning she transported them to her former son-in-law's house for the weekend.

The divorce had left her unfettered by her daughter's marriage, so she could see her grandchildren as much as she liked. She could also become the kind of grandmother she wanted to be. She described herself as "more of an Auntie Mame—they think I'm the funniest woman in the world." She devoted considerable thought to activities that would keep them entertained. She described one popular weekend: "I pick them up on Friday after work. We go to the Pizza Hut for dinner—then home to watch TV. I keep lots of goodies around for them. They fight. I shush them. Then they zonk out. The next morning, I fix breakfast—they watch TV. Then I take them to their dad's and dump them. It's kinda nice."

Her grandchildren have provided an important source of her identity. When asked what they do for her, she replied, "I feel that I am alone, and they give me stability. For example, some of the old maids at work look lonely—they have nothing. I always have something to look forward to. They are good for me. I feel of some worth." By our third contact, her grandchildren were in their teens, and her grandson was in serious trouble—he had been arrested for selling drugs. Mrs. Earlham felt that both parents were too absorbed in their own problems to deal with their son's: "I'll have a stroke or heart attack before these grandchildren grow up." She described how much tension she felt about these problems, so much so that it was interfering with her work: "I get really upset and sick inside." She considered herself to be unlike most grandmothers, who, in her view, "have bleached hair, are overpainted, self-centered, and so engrossed in themselves." Instead, "I am the one who is always there. I am the most stable figure in their lives. I take them out to dinner. I buy them clothes. Most important, I bother about them." In fact, she was the only one who was aware of her granddaughter's first menstrual period and who instructed her on what it entailed.

Over the time of the research, her grandchildren passed into adolescence. With their new distractions, the Friday night get-togethers became only intermittent. Mrs. Earlham was resigned to their behavioral problems and reported she would love them "no matter what." She has had her rewards.

They have their own interests now, but I feel really good about them. My granddaughter wrote a paper at school saying that I was the most memorable person she had ever known because I took her places and told her about her mother as a child. She said she couldn't imagine her life without me. My grandson also wrote a paper about me, saying he could really talk to me, that I understood him and I made him feel good about himself. My friends at work criticize me for doing too much for my grandchildren. But one can never do too much.

Mrs. Robinson's grandparenting is in sharp contrast to Mrs. Earlham's. She is a widow in her late sixties who went back to school after retirement. She sold her suburban home and bought a small cottage near the beach. Most of her interests center on her volunteer work with retarded children and on her weaving. After a long and unhappy marriage, she was clearly enjoying her freedom and independence. She described her family in a soft-spoken and nonemotional manner. Mrs. Robinson had maintained distant but friendly relationships with her four children, three of whom lived in the area and all of whom had been divorced and remarried. The notable thing about this extended family system is that Mrs. Robinson had also maintained friendly relationships with all of her former in-laws. In fact, she described these relationships with the same detachment with which she discussed her own children and grandchildren.

She saw her grandchildren only intermittently, particularly as they had entered college or the work world. She was hardly ever alone with them. Whenever they did come to visit, they would immediately go for a walk in the park. "There are few occasions for us to be together, and there is not too much to talk about," she said. Although the divorces of her children upset her and made her uncertain of her role, she concluded that in the long run the divorces have had little impact on her life. She had mixed feelings about her gradual withdrawal from her grandchildren's lives.

I've come to understand that our family permits each other a great deal of independence, particularly as we all get older. I want this independence, even if sometimes I want to call the tune. And I want to be coaxed to participate in their lives. It's different with my grandchildren than it is with my children though. I always felt a part of their lives. I don't really feel a sense of belonging to my grandchildren, even though they are someone I love. Children belong to their parents, and their rearing is the parents' responsibility.

I never thought about being a grandparent or that I couldn't wait to be a grandparent. It just happened. I'm not a nongrandmother. I do care about them, but I have no right to say how they should be raised or what hairstyle they have. I want to be included in their lives, but I don't want to know all about them. I don't want to worry about what they do. I try to establish the midpoint between being aloof and intrusive.

RESPONSES TO THE SEPARATION AND THE DIVORCE

In the first stage of the divorce process, most grandparents were not well informed on the quality of their child's marriage even if they were in frequent contact. Thus, upon learning that their child's marriage was dissolving, many described their response as one of shock and dismay. Only those who had always been intimate with their children became their confidants as the marriage was dissolving. Only 38 percent of the grandparents reported that their children had discussed their marital problems with them. Another 33 percent had vague hints that their children were not happy or that the relationship was breaking down. Other grandmothers had always respected the privacy of their child's nuclear family and suppressed any interest in what was occurring.

Upon learning of the actual separation, most grandmothers were surprised even though they may have sensed that something was wrong in their child's marital relationship. Some described themselves as stunned or shocked or distraught. "It was a shock. I lost sleep and cried a lot about it." "I was upset and angry at both of them." "I felt it could have worked out." "I was torn between my son and daughter-in-law. She has always been like a daughter to me." Often the emotional reaction reflected realistic concerns about the practical problems that they faced in assisting their children and grandchildren. For example, within a few weeks the Caughlins learned that both of their daughters' marriages were dissolving, affecting five grandchildren under the age of five. "When I first learned they were separating, I thought, 'Oh, my God, five kids to raise. They can't do it without our help.'"

Two-thirds of the grandparents had approved of the marriage initially, so most of them had maintained an amiable relationship with their son-in-law or daughter-in-law. Over one-third of the grandmothers regretted the divorce and in many instances complained of feelings of loss and sadness at the prospect of losing a child-in-law. In fact, to avoid such a loss, some grandmothers retained frequent contact even though their relationship with the in-law was formally severed with the divorce. In some cases, this tie continued because "my daughter-in-law is the parent of my grandchildren." In other cases, a genuine friendship had developed, which neither the grandmother nor her child-in-law wanted to dissolve. These women deemphasized the blood tie and included in-laws in their definition of family.

Identifying Causes

Most grandmothers were able to identify why a child's marriage ended. Although they might have been surprised when the separation occurred, they professed some knowledge of their child's marital problems, even if these were hindsight observations. The causes they identified were quite similar to those discussed by their children, except grandmothers were less aware of sexual problems. They were quite sensitive, however, to the personality and lifestyle differences they had observed in their child and his or her partner. Generally, grandmothers gave various explanations for the failure of the marriage either singly or in combination. Flaws in character or behavior of individuals were commonly mentioned: "They were too young and immature when they got married. Then the children came too fast." "They had financial difficulties, which placed a strain on them." "He was fanatically neat—always after her to be more orderly." Or, "They came from such different backgrounds."

The grandmothers, like their divorcing children, often concluded that the causes of divorce were vague and related to relational or personality factors, which eventually undermined the marriage: "They were incompatible—too different. She was incredibly stubborn, and he was incredibly stupid to go to a lawyer too impetuously." "He was traveling a lot. As a distraction, she got into est or something. They were never together." "They didn't love each other—they put each other down so much they could never grow in the relationship." "They were too busy—they didn't see enough of each other."

Grandmothers also identified broader social forces in the society that they felt influenced the life-styles of their children: "It has changed so much. They don't marry for life anymore. I guess we're lucky ours got married at all." Most grandmothers had not felt they had the right to leave an unhappy marriage. Many complained of their own toleration of marital unhappiness: "We stuck it out. We took more from each other." "We had more guts; the younger generation gets out instead of working to make a marriage stick."

Although their explanations for the divorce included some criticisms of their child and their former child-in-law, many grandmothers were hesitant to assign blame. These women tended to relate marital problems to the immutable forces in society or to the temperaments of the individuals: "They were temperamentally unsuitable to each other." "There were such differences in their upbringing—different values." "Women's liberation influenced her and my son wouldn't budge."

The vagueness of these remarks indicates that most grandparents were "intimate at a distance" while their child's marriage was intact. The privacy of their child's nuclear household was usually scrupulously observed even if the grandparents were aware of conflict, alcoholism, drug abuse, or great personal unhappiness. Once the marriage dissolved, the boundaries became more easily crossed, which potentially caused great change in the parent-child relationship. As one grandmother explained, "We couldn't help her while she was married. It was none of our business. But once they separated, we could help her get a car. I took the children until she found a good babysitter, and we helped to pay her rent."

THE NORMS OF GRANDPARENTING

The grandmothers in this research were quite sensitive, not only to the needs of their children and grandchildren, but also to the wishes of their children as to what should be done. When grandmothers were asked what they should do when a child divorces, they promptly detailed a list of rules that they used to regulate their activities with their grandchildren. In a content analysis of these responses, it was found that the grandmothers usually juxtaposed prescriptions with proscriptions and weighed what they should and should not do. The following list is revealing in understanding the extent to which their role is norm-directed (Johnson 1983a).

Prescriptions	*Proscriptions*
Be there	Don't interfere
Be an advocate	Don't buy love
Provide family continuity	Don't give advice
Be loving	Don't be too protective
Be a liaison with parents	Don't discipline
Be a source of security	Don't be a fuddy-duddy
Make it easier for parents	Don't expect too much
Babysit	Don't nag
Just enjoy them	Don't be dull
Be fun to be with	Don't be old-fashioned

The contrasts between the proscriptive and prescriptive norms are noticeable. In an examination of the prescriptions, the "shoulds" these grandmothers observe, one sees that they define their role as someone who can be the grandchild's advocate and intervene as a mediator with the parent. Moreover, they see themselves as a somewhat ambiguous, senior family member who is simply "there" to love the child, to provide security and a sense of family and its continuity. In this capacity of "being there," their mere presence provides them with the opportunity to observe, support, and indulge grandchildren, and in the process, to enhance the grandchild's self-esteem. Finally, as reported elsewhere (Neugarten and Weinstein 1964), a grandmother should be someone who is "fun to be with." It should be noted that, with the exception of babysitting, the grandmothers tended to assign vague and ambiguous prescriptive norms to their role.

On the whole, discussions of "should nots" involved more lengthy descriptions of specific rules for behavior. A grandmother should not interfere, she should not give too much advice, and she should not discipline grandchildren. She must not overprotect or spoil a grandchild or, worse yet, attempt to buy love. She should not be old-fashioned or outdated, nor should she nag or be judgmental. Lastly, she should not be disappointed if the grandchildren do not return the favors; she cannot expect too much.

The proscriptive norms were more frequently mentioned in the interviews, and discussions were lengthier and more detailed. These "should nots" are in keeping with a strong norm of non-interference. In contrast, prescriptions, or the "shoulds," were usually passed over quickly. The grandmothers appear to have more explicit conceptions of what they should not do than of what they should do. A grandmother can more easily avoid "buying love" than she can attempt to "enhance self-esteem." She can avoid interfering more easily than she can provide a sense of family continuity. She can probably alleviate her disappointments with grandchildren through other activities without too much difficulty. If a grandmother views herself mainly as a love object, however, there are few specific guidelines for action.

A second source of evidence was a questionnaire that explored the degree to which the grandparent role is normatively directed. To address this question, we examined transcripts of the first interviews for comments commonly made about grandparenting, which were then incorporated into a twenty-item questionnaire. The twenty items covered three categories suggestive of grandparenting norms. First, contrary to some interpretations (Troll 1982), most grandmothers had clear conceptions of their role. They defined it as voluntary and specialized in social and emotional functions rather than instrumental ones. They conceptualized a preferred relationship with their grandchildren that was more of a friendship than a hierarchical intergenerational relationship. Almost three-quarters agreed with the statement, "These days grandparents and grandchildren are more like friends." Also in keeping with this type of relationship, most grandmothers said they had no difficulty finding things to talk about with grandchildren or in keeping them entertained (Johnson 1988a).

Second, most respondents drew clear boundaries between parenting and grandparenting, viewing each role as quite distinct in its functions. For example, these grandmothers had few uncertainties about what they should do. The majority concluded that they had some influence over grandchildren, but not because of specific actions on their part. A majority agreed that they did not want to repeat the parent role and instead preferred to be with their grandchildren on a voluntary and short-term basis. The only parenting function they favored was that of disciplining grandchildren in their own home. Although they felt they had some influence over their grandchildren, that influence did not come under the guise of parenting. Few viewed grandparenting as a second chance at parenting or felt grandparenting was more enjoyable than the earlier parenting of their own children. Consistent with the friendshiplike character of the preferred role, only 11 percent of the grandmothers felt that they should inculcate moral standards in their grandchildren.

Third, the grandparent role was most often viewed as secondary and less important than other roles. Only two grandmothers agreed with the statement, "I am one of those people whose life revolves around my grandchildren"; while less than one-third agreed with, "I like to see my grandchildren more than anything I can think of." Only 26 percent reported that they enjoyed their grandchildren more than they had enjoyed their own children when they were young. Other things in life appeared to be more satisfying for most of these women, so their grandchildren were not as likely to play a role in combating loneliness.

Because age and kinship relationship were such important determinants of these grandmothers' contacts with and supports for grandchildren, their responses were broken down by these variables. In regard to the age of the grandmother, only one significant age difference was found in the responses. Older grandmothers were much more likely to agree with the comment "I have very little influence over my grandchildren," a finding that most likely reflects their actual or perceived distance from their grandchildren. The kinship relationship appears to have had little effect on the grandmothers' perceptions of their role; there were no significant differences in responses of maternal grandmothers and those of paternal grandmothers. Although maternal grandmothers were more actively involved with their grandchildren, these women were in basic agreement with paternal grandmothers on the norms of grandparenting.

These findings are consistent with findings from a survey of grandparents in a more conservative, middle western, middle-class sample (Aldous 1985). For those respondents, grandparenting was only one of the numerous activities in their lives, and they tended to reject becoming parents to grandchildren. It appears, then, that ideally for most, grandchildren are to be loved and enjoyed but are not in need of parenting. The expectations for grandparenting of the women in this sample were quite distinct from parenting; for them, grandparenting is a voluntary, part-time role specializing in social and emotional functions and secondary to other roles.

Age Norms and Grandparenting Styles

Open-ended discussions also documented the agreement of grand-mothers in their conceptions of the role. They used a traditional type of grandmother as a standard against which they could redefine and modify their own role. This grandmother type is drawn from the past and bears a close resemblance to the songs and stories of childhood. The popular Thanksgiving song that begins, "Over the river and through the woods to grandmother's house we go" provides thematic material for this conception. Most people would agree with one respondent's image of the traditional grandmother: "I see her as a fat old woman, white hair on top of her head. She wears an apron and is always at the stove baking cookies or preparing large meals." Others see the grandmother in another old-fashioned setting: "She is someone sitting in a rocking chair by the fire with a shawl over her shoulders, a kindly, doting woman." This prototype of the grandmother is one who is old, nurturing, and maternal, and who can at least selectively offer warmth, shelter, and security to her grandchildren (Johnson 1983a).

Most women in the study rejected this image of a grandmother because she is too narrow and domestic and has no life outside the family. One woman noted, "She never goes out—she is not much fun." Since they usually described the preferred type of grand-mother as someone whom grandchildren want to visit, not someone they are obligated to visit, the respondents agreed that she should be fun-loving—a requirement the traditional grand-mother cannot fulfill. As one respondent put it: "Being kindly and doting doesn't fill the bill with today's grandchildren. She must be the type that makes her grandchildren happy." To do so, many grandmothers felt that they should be a friend, a pal, or a play-mate. "For my generation, our grandmothers were not much fun. They could never cope with today's children."

Most grandmothers also disassociated themselves from the traditional image because they considered themselves too young. A few quotes will illustrate this repeated theme: "I'm too young to be a grandmother." "I'm just not the grandmother type—I travel, I take courses, I have my own interests." "I have my own life to lead; so do my grandchildren." "Just because I'm a grandmother doesn't mean I am old." Implicit in their rejection of the traditional type was their association of grandparenthood with old age. In some cases, the rejection of the traditional grandmother type bordered on gerontophobia.

As a modern grandmother who is the image of youth, this fun-loving person devises activities that will make the grandchildren happy. Instead of working over the stove all day or being a "cookie-baking grandmother," she takes them to Burger King or McDonalds' and lets them eat what they choose. "I'm turning them into fast-food junkies," one grandmother reported. Instead of watching Lawrence Welk on television, she liked "Fonzie" and their other favorite programs. One grandmother aptly summarized how the traditional image has been revised; she referred to herself as the Pied Piper whom the grandchildren follow in a round of swimming and trips to the zoo, Disneyland, and ball games. Another described herself as the "city grandmother" who takes her grandchildren to I. Magnin, art galleries, or the ballet, while the other grandmother is the "country grandmother" who retains the traditional features of the role. Another woman, who lived in an age-segregated community, described the modern grandmother as "well coiffed and manicured who, over the bridge table sighs and says, 'Thank God my grandchildren have gone home.'"

These modern women have concluded that they can confine themselves to fun-loving activities because their role is not only optional but also without major authority functions: "Let the parents do the directing. I just enjoy them." "Being a grandparent has all the good parts—have them over when you choose and send them home when they act bratty. And you don't have to nurse them through an illness." "When they are good, I love it. When they are bad, I send them home."

Thus, the image of a grandmother has changed from the kindly old woman secluded in her home to a lively middle-aged woman who leads an active and interesting life. She easily accepts the responsibilities of grandparenting because they are only temporary and intermittently imposed. Moreover, she has rejected any authority functions in order to retain her friendly, fun-loving image. Her style, then, rests upon the satisfaction not only of her grandchildren's needs for pleasure but also those of her own. While most of the grandmothers preferred this arrangement, the absence of responsibility also resulted in greater distance. One grandmother noted: "I am not very close to them because I'm not responsible for them. They are not my problem, so I don't butt in."

The Meaning of Grandparenthood and Family Role Models

In the design of the interview format, there was some difficulty in finding questions that elicited an individual's conception of grandparenthood. One question—How do you picture yourself as a grandparent?—repeatedly elicited the response "I have never thought about it." Most respondents clearly had not consciously conceptualized themselves as grandparents before the birth of grandchildren; after becoming grandparents, they rarely subjected their actions to critical self-reflection. In the absence of specific guidelines, many grandmothers described their actions as spontaneous and situationally determined—"I just roll with the punches" or "I just take it as it comes."

In an attempt to probe further into the meanings of grandparenthood, questions were added about respondents' own grandmothers. Although these questions were not asked on the original 20 percent of the interviews, the remainder provide insights into preparation for the grandparent role. For example, 58 percent had not known a grandmother or had only seen her on rare occasions. In numerous cases, their grandmothers had remained in Europe when their parents immigrated to the United States. Other families had moved to the West Coast, leaving their parents in the East or Midwest, so the opportunities for contact were rare. Of the remainder, who saw their own grandmother during childhood (42 percent of the sample), only one-half had positive memories of her. In the remaining half, the grandmothers were described negatively as "Victorian," "prudish," "senile," or "too old."

Almost two-thirds of the grandmothers reported that their mothers had been active grandmothers with their children. The remainder had mothers who had either died before the birth of their children or had lived at too great a distance to play a meaningful role. Of the 65 percent whose own mothers had been active as grandmothers, only 38 percent described them with affection and admiration. The remaining respondents described a negative relationship with their own mothers that prevented their mothers from functioning as their role models. One can conclude that only a minority of today's grandmothers had experience with grandmothers within their own families. Early deaths, immigrant background, and geographic mobility had prevented these women from forming conceptions of the role based upon personal experience. Moreover, where their own mothers and grandmothers had been active in the role of grandmother, their actions were not viewed positively.

Because of the lack of positive role models, most women were only weakly socialized into the role. Such a situation has several implications. Most importantly, without role models, individuals are likely to use personal definitions of the role. Because the role is not regulated by expectations transmitted from generation to generation, grandmothers can mold their role to suit their own life-style. Moreover, without role models, grandmothers probably can more easily adapt to the more permissive values and life-styles of their children and grandchildren. Such a flexible approach would not be possible if they were guided by the traditional models of the past.

Responses to Divorce

Despite the specificity of their norms of grandparenting, when presented with the divorce of an offspring and the opportunity to substitute for parents in meeting the basic needs of the grandchildren, the grandmothers in this sample were somewhat confused about their potential functions. They tended to define their role on an ad hoc basis depending upon the needs of the situation. Most grandmothers determined the level of their involvement situationally depending on the needs of their children, grandchildren, and even children-in-law.

Some grandmothers identified few specific functions they felt they should perform (Johnson 1983a), usually following the practice of one respondent: "I just sit back and observe and then try to do what I can." Others viewed themselves as "stabilizers" and described their home as an island of security in the shifting confusions in the lives of their children and grandchildren. As one respondent summarized this function, "The grandchildren know I am always here and my door is always open to them." Still others reported they were confidants, "someone who has time to listen to them and sit back and observe their lives." Finally, about one-fourth became parental surrogates to grandchildren, situations that will be described below. With these exceptions, conceptions rarely depicted a grandmother who would intervene. Instead, she was described as passive, supportive by her mere presence.

REDEFINITIONS OF THE ROLE
WITH DIVORCE

Throughout our discussions, grandmothers had clear conceptions of what they should not do; but they expressed problems identifying who was responsible for determining what they should do to assist their child's family. Neither the parent nor the grandparent, nor, for that matter, the grandchild, were delegated the chief responsibility for determining a grandmother's actions. Since their most specific norms centered on noninterference in their child's family, grandmothers generally concluded that their relationship with a grandchild was voluntary, so it had to be personally negotiated and situationally defined. Although the relationship was achieved through their own efforts, they did not generally see themselves as operating as free agents. Any actions they took were potentially constrained by the parents, only one of whom was a blood relative.

The major dilemma facing these grandmothers was commonly expressed with ambivalence: "If I do too much, I will have to do it all. If I do too little, I might lose them." This response reflected the quandary created by the voluntary character of the role in a situation when needs were high. If the decision was made to take over parenting functions, grandmothers felt that they faced the risk of becoming overburdened. Since there were only vague and often implicit expectations for the role, grandmothers in general were hesitant to intervene, particularly when their responsibilities were not clearly delimited. Explanations often entailed a rationalization that the parent role should not be repeated: "I have paid my dues. It is time for me to think of myself."

Grandmothers also evaluated their role in terms of principles of exchange and calculated the costs and rewards accruing to them. In response to the question "What do your grandchildren do for you?" most grandmothers pointed to the reciprocal exchange of love. The relationship with grandchildren was often described as a "pure" relationship that, unlike the relationship with a child, had indeterminate rights and obligations: "It's a deeper love than between a parent and child because it is coming from a loved one [a child] and the result of loving and being loved." Given a relationship in which love was perceived as the primary exchange commodity, it was not surprising that the perceived rewards also were intangible. Underlying their evaluation of the cost-reward balance were psychological benefits such as enhanced self-esteem, genetic continuity, and an intimate relatedness to a young child.

From this perspective of a voluntary relationship with nebulous rewards, the cost side of the ledger in large part was controlled by the grandmother as she voluntarily constricted and expanded her activities with her grandchildren. A major contingency, however, was beyond her control: she faced the possibility of rejection. The fear of rejection was indirectly expressed by a refusal to take the initiative in easing the strains of divorce. Many grandmothers described themselves as noninterfering: "I just tiptoe around and attempt to pick up the pieces." One advised, "Don't try to do too much and then you won't be hurt."

Age, Kinship Link, and Intergenerational Involvement

However hesitant they are about conceptualizing their role, in reality, most grandmothers rise to the occasion and extend assistance to their children and their grandchildren. To review previous publications on the responses of grandmothers soon after their child's divorce was finalized, a large majority were in at least weekly contact with their children (Johnson 1983a; Johnson 1985a; Johnson 1988a; Johnson and Barer 1987). While these grandmothers had less contact with grandchildren than with their children, they were actively assisting in the period immediately following divorce. A large majority also provided financial help and most provided some services at least intermittently.

Table 5.1 reports on the responses of the grandmothers in this study both at our first contact and at our final contact about forty months later. Initially the age of the grandmother was the variable that most clearly determined the frequency of contact. Younger grandmothers had significantly more contact with grandchildren than those sixty-five and older. Most women were "on-time" as grandparents, having had their children in their twenties and thirties. Thus, younger women had younger grandchildren, who needed more support after divorce than did teen-age grandchildren. The older grandmothers had older grandchildren, who were relatively independent and in less need of help. The younger women were not only more active in family activities, but also were more likely to be married and working.

The kinship relationship, the maternal or paternal linkage, was a less significant determinant of grandparenting activities at Time 1 than was age, although paternal grandmothers did have less

Table 5.1
Changes in Grandparenting (N = 43)

	Over Time	
	Time One	*Time Two*
Contact—weekly or more (by percentage)		
Adult child	74	65
Grandchildren	60	53
Former child-in-law	19	12
Assistance (by means)		
Economic	2.5	1.3
Services	3.8	3.3
Social/emotional	6.4	5.2*

	By Age of Grandmother			
	Under 65		*65 and over*	
	Time 1	*Time 2*	*Time 1*	*Time 2*
Contact—weekly or more (by percentage)				
Adult child	79	67	70	63
Grandchildren	75	63	35	42
Former child-in-law	25	17	12	11
Assistance (by means)				
Economic	3.0	1.5	1.9	1.2
Services	5.4	4.9	1.9	1.3
Social/emotional	7.2	5.4*	5.3	5.0

	By Kinship Relationship			
	Maternal		*Paternal*	
	Time 1	*Time 2*	*Time 1*	*Time 2*
Contact—weekly or more (by percentage)				
Adult child	78	72	73	57
Grandchild	65	68	53	38
Former child-in-law	9	5	32	23

Assistance (by means)				
Economic	1.8	1.4	2.1	1.3*
Services	4.0	4.1	3.1	2.6*
Social/emotional	6.3	6.8	6.0	4.4*

*T-test, $p = < .05$ between times and within each age group

contact with their grandchildren than did maternal grandmothers. They also were less active in providing help to them. Few of their sons had custody, so many mothers of sons maintained contact with their former daughters-in-law, who in turn provided them access to their grandchildren.

Comparisons of the extent of involvement of grandmothers over the months these women were followed show there was some decline in the grandmothers' contact with children, grandchildren, and children-in-law (Johnson 1988a). In the supports grandmothers provided to their children and grandchildren, there was also a decline over time, although none of these changes were statistically significant. Age differences in involvement over time continued, with younger women having more contact with grandchildren at both points of time. The age of the grandmother was also an important determinant of the assistance grandmothers provided. Younger women provided significantly more services than older women at both points in time.

The kinship relationship was also an important determinant of variations in the grandmothers' responses over the period of the research. At Time 1, the differences between the activities of maternal and paternal grandmothers were not impressive. By our final contact, however, paternal grandmothers had significantly less contact with grandchildren, and they provided significantly fewer social and emotional supports to their children and grandchildren.

To summarize, the findings suggest that grandparenting is primarily a middle-age activity, at least as evaluated by social contact and services. The instrumental component of their role was quite prominent among those grandmothers who had responsibility for young grandchildren. Relationships with children did not vary significantly, a finding that indicates that it is the grandparent role, not the parent role, that is subject to the most variation. The real decline in involvement was found among paternal grandmothers. Since the grandmother's role is derived through her relationship with her child, one can conclude that sons are less able to sustain their mothers' relationship to their children than are daughters.

Correlates to Satisfaction with Grandparenting

Grandparenting activities following a child's divorce are determined in large part by factors beyond the grandmother's control. Other research suggests that they have a derived role in which their access to grandchildren is determined by the parents of their grandchildren (Furstenberg 1981). For example, most grandparents cannot enter their grandchildren's home unannounced or take grandchildren to movies without first arranging these activities with their parents. Thus, their actions are to a large part determined by the grandchildren's parents.

It is also important to examine the relationship between grandparents and their adult children, because it may affect grandparenting activities. Respondents in both generations identified dimensions of the relationships in pen-and-paper tests. In regard to the grandparent generation, over half the women were satisfied with their role of grandmother at both points in time, and about the same proportion were also satisfied with their divorcing child's situation. When correlations were run for associations between their satisfaction with their family roles and other factors, interesting findings emerged. Being satisfied with the role of grandmother was associated with a relatively unproblematic and nonconflictual relationship with the divorcing child. More satisfaction with the grandparent role was found in those families where the adult child and grandchildren were having few problems in their adaptation following divorce and in those where the grandmother was providing significant support.

The divorcing children also filled in a written questionnaire on these subjects. About half of them at both points in time were satisfied with their mothers and grandmothers. Almost 40 percent reported a "very close" relationship with their mother, and slightly fewer reported the relationship was unproblematic. Almost half reported life would be harder without their parents in the area. The results of correlations run between their satisfaction with their mother and other variables were similar to those for the grandmothers. They suggest that relationships between generations best function in an unproblematic environment. Divorced individuals' positive reports on their relationship with their parents were associated with their satisfaction with them as grandparents and with their having consensus on childrearing techniques. These favorable reports also were associated with the respondents having fewer problems in adaptation and reporting fewer problems in their children's adaptation. Parents usually provided high supports in these cases, but their adult children were also actively involved in friendship and dating networks.

The Role of Grandfathers

Although this research did not focus specifically on grandfathers, they were present in 69 percent of the families. A number of men were interviewed, and in other families, their wives and children reported on their activities with grandchildren. Several findings are worth noting here. First, grandfathers tended to be active with grandchildren only if their wives were active. For example, among paternal grandparents, if a grandmother maintained a close relationship with a former child-in-law, the grandfather, too, was more involved than were those where no such bond developed.

Second, the grandfathers over sixty-five were no more active with grandchildren than were younger ones. Even with more leisure time, only 20 percent of these older men were active with grandchildren in comparison to 27 percent of the younger men. In all, only nine men were in frequent contact with grandchildren and took over fathering functions. Of these, six were retired, most of whom were under sixty-five. Unlike the middle-aged grandmothers who worked and were also actively engaged with grandchildren, most middle-aged grandfathers were invested in their careers and quite remote from their grandchildren. Few grandfathers in the sample participated in activities with grandchildren independently from their wives. Similar findings were found with a larger, more diverse sample (Kivett 1985). Grandfathers, however, did emphasize the economic and instrumental functions at all ages. Many men were vigilant protectors of children's economic interests during the divorce process, and many men assisted their children in rearranging their economic affairs after the divorce.

DISCREPANCIES BETWEEN
EXPECTATIONS AND REALITIES

At one level of the analysis, the grandparenting styles of our respondents were quite similar to those identified previously (Cherlin and Furstenberg 1986; Neugarten and Weinstein 1964; Robertson 1977). On the one hand, there was the distant grandmother who maintained little contact or reciprocity with her children or grandchildren. Some of the women in the study were remote and formal grandmothers who justified this distance on the basis of a lack of common interests or because of competing commitments. Other distant grandmothers spoke of their role with great sentimentality, but in reality they had little contact with grandchildren and provided them with very little assistance. As their written questionnaires indicate, most grandmothers in this sample preferred a fun-loving role that stressed social and recreational functions.

Of particular interest, then, are those grandmothers who felt impelled to actions that were inconsistent with their expectations for a more fun-loving role (Johnson 1988a). Approximately one-third of the grandmothers provided all types of assistance to their children and grandchildren over the forty months we followed these families. Unlike those who withdrew their assistance because a child remarried, a grandchild moved away, or new childcare arrangements were made, those with long-term involvement assumed a parentlike role on a more permanent basis.

The women with long-term involvements were usually younger grandmothers responding to the needs of young grandchildren. For example, one mother had abandoned her infant, leaving a distraught young father whose mother was forced to take over full-time care of her grandson. By doing so, she actually prevented placement of her grandson in a foster home. In several other cases, men had abandoned their wives, who were left with limited financial resources on which to raise young children. In those cases and others, grandmothers felt a strong responsibility to alleviate these serious stressors. As the grandmothers reacted to these crises, their role was no longer voluntary, flexible, and focused on recreational and expressive functions. These women were responsible for the care and protection of grandchildren—pressures inconsistent with their conceptions of the preferred role. Instead of becoming fun-loving friends who focused on recreational activities, they were forced to become disciplinarians and the monitors of the grandchildren's health and well-being.

Since becoming surrogate parents was incongruent with their expectations, it is not surprising that these women expressed considerable ambivalence about their role. Many insisted, "I never wanted to repeat the parent role." They were particularly uncomfortable about having to discipline grandchildren. They also complained about the blurring of boundaries between the roles of parent and grandparent. For example, one grandmother described her full-time responsibilities for a five-year-old grandson. She made clear distinctions between her role as a parent and her role as a grandparent and concluded they were inherently incompatible. She explained: "I am the only one who sees that he gets his vitamins, that he has a normal life, that he gets to bed on time, that he doesn't run wild. Because of all that, I can never be a grand-mother. I can't indulge him like I do my other grandchildren. I have to discipline him, so I can't be fun to be around."

A full-time commitment to grandchildren also has repercussions on the relationship with an adult child. Generally, the intact family (before a child's divorce) was private, and many actions of its members were not observable by grandparents. With divorce, that level of privacy often ended if divorcing parents were forced to turn to their parents for help. As grandparents became actively involved on a day-to-day basis, they also became familiar with large areas of their child's life, which previously had been closed to them. Such familiarity was not usually welcomed by either genera-tion, and it created an especially ambiguous situation for grandpar-ents. In some cases, grandparents had to deal with an adult child's increased immaturity, blurring the boundaries between age groups. In other cases, adult children enlisted their parents as best friends and confidants, disclosing information on the most private areas of their lives. In such cases, the age and generation bound-aries were easily crossed.

Role and Boundary Confusions

Important conceptual issues arise regarding the norms that make distinctions between the roles of grandparent, parent, and child. For one thing, age norms deem which actions are appropriate or inappropriate to one's age. I assume that where age norms are specified explicitly, these form normative boundaries between generations. In one type of family, parents, grandparents, and grandchildren tended to distinguish clear boundaries between generations and expected differing actions from each other. In other families, there was a tendency to blur such distinctions. Grandparents deemphasized old-age norms and wanted to be friendly companions to grandchildren. Still others tended to preserve age norms and maintain remote and formal relationships. Grandmothers, in any case, expressed considerable ambivalence about their situation when boundaries became blurred between their roles of parent and grandparent.

Phenomenologically, some respondents held expectations for family members based on age and generation status in the family. They maintained that parents should behave differently than their children. In such cases any variance from expectations drew critical comments. Age norms were particularly prominent: "She is acting like a child." "My mother is forgetting her age." "My son treats me like a friend—too much so. I don't want to hear about his sex life." In other words, if one diverged too far from the expectations of the role, others disapproved. These families can be contrasted to others where age and generation distinctions were blurred. The ideal parent-child relationship was often equated to friendship, while the grandparent-grandchild relationship was ideally considered a fun-loving one.

With divorce, these distinctions between age and generation units often change because the norm of privacy of the nuclear unit weakens. From the grandparents' perspective, when a child is married, the child's roles of spouse and parent normatively take precedence over the relationship with a parent. Both parents and their adult children agreed here. Generally, grandmothers in the sample scrupulously respected the privacy of their children's family life. A divorced child has, of course, abandoned the spousal role, an action that has a direct impact on relationships between generations. It permits both parents and their divorcing children to move easily across the generational boundaries.

To summarize this chapter and the diverse patterns and themes found, I should first emphasize that the grandmothers' responses to their children's divorces were quite varied, not only because of the variables of age and kinship relationship, but also because the norms of grandparenting were somewhat blurred and ambiguous. The meanings, or the cultural content, of the role, however, were quite uniform: most grandmothers rejected the traditional conceptions of the role and its nurturing elements. Where they identified more explicit directives, they were more concerned about what they should not do than about what they should do.

Nevertheless, the help they extended to children and grandchildren was impressive. Grandparents provided resources that were held in reserve until needed. When grandmothers were forced to take on parenting functions, however, they invariably did so with great reservations. As most defined the role in terms of friendly, fun-loving activities, they found it difficult to be a grandparent if they also had to take over parenting responsibilities. The highest needs most often arose with younger grandchildren, so the grandparents who were most involved were also younger.

As the foregoing indicates, the divorce process engenders changes in the roles of parent and grandparent. After accounting for the strong effect the variable of age has on grandparenting, I conclude that the long-term relationship with one's child is also a significant determinant of the role. For many, divorce strengthens the bond between generations. In such situations, the grandparents often heard their child's complaints of a failing marriage. They could assume a supportive family role because their relationship had always been interdependent. Then the grandchildren were beneficiaries. In other families, grandparents continued to be remote after the divorce. In still other cases, grandparents adopted the new order and joined in a network of new and former in-laws; in the process, they could pick up additional grandchildren.

Irrespective of the form of reorganization after divorce, most grandmothers rejected the traditional dimensions of their role. They much preferred being a youngish Auntie Mame who was there to have fun with grandchildren. They avoided disciplining or attempting to transmit moral values—tasks they felt were better left to parents. Thus, they strove to preserve boundaries between parenting and grandparenting. Another prominent finding in the foregoing concerns less the grandparents' objective activities than the subjective meanings of these activities. As products of our culture, grandparents also have adopted the values of this region of the country at this point in history and thus are quite resistant to making sacrifices for children and grandchildren.

◇ 6 ◇

PARENTS AND
THEIR ADULT CHILDREN

THE sentimentality so often noted in regard to grandparents and grandchildren is rarely observed in the relationship between adults and their parents. It is possible that the idealization of grandparents is an attempt to defuse tensions in relationships between parents and adult children. The cruel stepmother of fairy tales and myths is only a thinly disguised expression of the negative side of the image of mother. Some years ago, a social critic proposed the term *momism* to refer to the mothering of "a generation of vipers" (Wylie 1979). Such pejorative remarks on occasion outweigh the countervailing image that sentimentally equates motherhood with God and country.

In comparison to research on parents and young children, there are few studies of the parent-child relationship in later stages of the family cycle. One exception is the literature with a developmental perspective, which uses such concepts as cohort, generational, and lineage (Hagestad 1981; Troll and Bengtson 1979). The "generation gap" is another area of widespread interest. Rather than "gaps," however, studies suggest there are strong ties between parents and children and close and nonconflictual relationships (Cicirelli 1983a; Troll 1982; Troll and Bengtson 1979). While these studies present intriguing interpretations, particularly of the two-way effects in intergenerational relations, the concepts and findings do not have great explanatory power for the interactional dynamics observed in my research. In fact, parent–adult child relationships observed in these Northern California families were more like those described by Hess and Waring (1978), who suggest "rethinking the relationship." These authors cut through the common idealistic conceptions of this relationship to itemize the impressive constraints on positive relationships between generations.

Also relevant to my research findings are insights from clinical research that help to identify the subjective sense of attachment that characterizes the relationship between adults and their parents (Cohler 1983). Psychoanalytic perspectives emphasize the strong emotional bond between parent and child, which can persist even when the relationship is remote or conflictual (Boszormenyi-Nagy and Sparks 1973). The relationship also can persist involuntarily at the emotional level because it is so firmly embedded in the unconscious structure of the personality. Kahana and Levin (1971) have concluded that many psychological problems in adults can be traced to the failure to achieve mature independence from parents. Even in relatively mature relationships, children may experience intense guilt for having overthrown parental authority. However, the flow of resentment in the relationship is not unidirectional —from children to parents; clinicians report that, beyond the overt expressions of sentiments of love and commitment, many older parents express considerable ambivalence about their relationships with their children. In other words, both parents and children carry around an accumulation of emotions that even at a latent level can lead to intrapersonal and interpersonal conflict.

Such differing and often contradictory interpretations of the nature of commitment between parents and adult children demonstrate that with the exception of developmental perspectives based upon earlier parent-child relationships, there is no comprehensive theoretical approach to analyzing later stages in the relationship. A number of questions arise. Is the bond between parent and adult child more productively explored with psychoanalytic theory and the view that interaction is colored by its unique roots in the situation of infantile dependence (Cohler and Grunebaum 1981)? Or is the parent-child relationship best approached as a social relationship and interpreted with the concepts of the social sciences? Or should one undertake a process-oriented analysis in which the more dynamic interactions between parent and adult child are mapped? This chapter and the next will draw upon the concepts of all three approaches in an analysis of the research findings on parents and their adult children during the divorce process. Because both generations were interviewed, the analysis can probe the degree of congruence between mothers and adult children as they explored their relationship through discussions with us.

ANALYZING OF INTERGENERATIONAL RELATIONSHIPS

After divorce, the parent-child relationship is often renegotiated. In earlier chapters, I categorized the families in this sample into three broad types according to how boundaries reformed after divorce. With a reemphasis on intergenerational bonds, parents and children strengthened their bond to each other. For many dyads, however, as later findings indicate, this arrangement was only temporary, lasting until the divorcing child had reorganized the nuclear family to adjust to the departure of a spouse.

I have suggested, however, that such an alternative is only possible because of existing resources that are potentially available in the parent–adult child relationship. If such resources are not available, then a divorcing individual has other alternatives. One alternative is to follow the lead of Susan Douglas (described in chapter 2), who as a single parent attempted to strengthen the resources in her nuclear household, retaining a fairly tight boundary that excluded her parents. With such a nuclear emphasis, a single parent and young children may assume an interdependence that blurs generational roles. In still other cases, the formerly married may construct a large and changeable network of blood relatives, in-laws, former in-laws, and friends, with loose and permeable boundaries around all units.

Given the freedom permitted in our kinship system, both parents and their children have the right to choose from various options. In a content analysis of the interviews, we found that at the manifest level the respondents were concerned with practical decisions such as determining the tasks to be performed and the occasions for interactions. These decisions ultimately determined the degree of intimacy or distance in the relationship and the nature of the reciprocity between generations. Both parents and their children also had to deal with status changes accompanying the increased dependency of adult children. Usually, with the dissolution of the adult child's nuclear household and the departure of a child-in-law, the boundary that had protected the privacy of the adult child's family became more permeable. As a result, more of the actions of the divorcing individual were subject to parental scrutiny. With one's life opened to parental purview and the sharing of confidences as parents stepped in to help out, household units became more open and public and family roles became blurred.

Decisions are based upon a host of variables. In addition to the socioeconomic and demographic characteristics typical in the suburban subculture in which the respondents live, key transition points also alter relationships. For example, scheduled life events based upon growth and development are one source of change in the nature of the tasks parents and children perform. In childhood, the relationship between parent and child is asymmetrical. Parents are in a superior position from which they control social and economic resources. Once a child leaves home and becomes economically self-supporting, there are pressures for symmetry in relationships, at least in middle-class families. When adult children themselves have children, the sharing of parenthood roles enhances this symmetry. As the parents approach advanced old age, a stage of filial maturity may be reached in which an adult child must extend help to parents rather than receive help from them.

Transitions also take place with unscheduled life events such as divorce, a time when both the nuclear family and the kinship unit change. In some cases, transitions in the divorcing individual may be regressive ones. For example, research on the mother-daughter relationship (Fischer 1981) has shown that a daughter's marriage and parenthood are points at which the relationship is renegotiated. Her status as an adult is affirmed, and any adolescent traits are left behind. One can assume that another turning point is reached following divorce, when the relationship can potentially revert back to a form similar to an earlier stage.

As with most transitions, revised expectations in the relationship can result in changes in patterns of reciprocity. The parent-child relationship is conventionally regulated by a diffuse sense of obligation, which, because of the diffuseness, covers broad areas of potential activities (Johnson 1978; Johnson 1983b). Generalized exchanges in which there is no direct accounting for debts and credits are the preferred patterns of reciprocity. In reality, most parents give far more to adult children than they receive in return (Sussman 1968), though a delayed repayment of the child's debts may be expected in a parent's old age. Neither generation, however, wants to be a burden on the other. At those points when either parents or children require more aid, patterns of reciprocity change. With divorce, for example, parents often must give far more in instrumental aid without necessarily receiving emotional benefits in return.

The relationship between parent and adult child also has a history and must be examined retrospectively. Any relationship between a parent and an adult child reflects earlier interactions and sentiments. From this perspective, the parent–adult child relationship accrues rather than changing meanings over time, because earlier emotional content is not forgotten. The following excerpts from interviews will illustrate how a history of conflict or ambivalence, on one hand, or delayed independence strivings of the child, on the other hand, although long ago resolved, become reactivated during the divorce process. Thus, although major transitions redefine the relationship, they also recapitulate, preserve, and revive the emotions and meanings attached to the relationship throughout its history.

THE EYES OF THE BEHOLDER:
VIEWS FROM EACH GENERATION

The problem of analyzing the parent-child relationship using data from both generations was probably best summarized by one man we interviewed. When asked about his relationship with his mother, he replied, "Which one—the one I have with her or the one she has with me?" The phenomenological branch of sociology describes these types of social data as "social constructions of reality." In navigating the social world, innumerable experiences of reality become shared, socially ordered, and consensually agreed upon. As Berger and Kellner point out, "The socially constructed world must be continually mediated and actualized by the individual, so that it can become and remain indeed his world as well" (1964, 179). Although their comment refers to the marital dyad, the parent and adult child do not necessarily share the same view of reality or have a consensual construction of their social relationship.

In comparing how parents and their adult children independently described to us their relationship with each other, we found inconsistencies that suggested the relationship was not always consensually validated. In some cases, perceptions were incongruent; while in others, it appeared that they were describing different relationships. A son might say, "I love her but I don't think she thinks I do," while his mother says, "He never appreciates me." A daughter says, "We disagree on almost everything," while her mother says, "We've become good friends since her divorce." Or a daughter describes her mother: "She wants us to be dependent on her in every way. She has never allowed us space to separate from her." Her mother responds to a similar question: "She's not in-dependent yet—imagine a mother of teenagers coming running to her mother with every little problem."

When parents and their adult children cannot reach a consensus in their perceptions of the relationship or act upon any inconsistencies they perceive, large areas of their lives are closed to each other. In some cases, partners in the dyad do not perceive important changes in the situation of the other. For example, a mother may not be sensitive to her daughter's new feelings of independence from her, or a son may be insensitive to his mother's desire for more freedom from family responsibilities. Irrespective of personal differences, parents and children differ in age and hence in historical experiences. As a result, they do not always share the same view of reality.

Paired comparisons of mothers and their divorcing children found that, on the whole, responses describing their relationships were quite similar on the more objective activities and behaviors. They differed significantly, however, in the expectations they had for each other, a finding that will be discussed in the next section. The children tended to identify more negative features of the relationship than their mothers did. For example, they reported more conflict with their mothers than mothers reported they had with their children. They also were more likely to perceive their mothers as more remote from their marital problems than their mothers felt they were. Children also tended to underreport economic help. Where it was given, they considered it as a debt, while their mothers tended to report that the money extended was a gift.

Because there are vague and sometimes conflicting norms regulating the parent-child relationship in our society, the interactions are not likely to show uniform patterns. As Merton and Barber (1963) point out, conflicting norms are not shown in behavior itself, but in oscillations in behavior, movements that are not necessarily experienced and recognized by both partners. Oscillations in behavior often entail opposing processes: the need to be dependent versus the desire to be independent, the urge to give versus the desire to hold, differing views on permissiveness or conformity, contradictory preferences for intimacy or detachment, and so on. Not surprisingly, then, there are often quite incongruent evaluations of the relationship.

LOWERING THE SHIELD OF PRIVACY

In keeping with the norm of noninterference, parents usually respected the privacy of a child's nuclear family as long as the child was married. As noted above, if a child turned to parents after a divorce, distance between generations decreased and boundaries between their households became more permeable. In the course of helping, parents had more opportunities to comment on their children's activities or to advise them on childrearing or running the household. Some parents became friends to their children, blurring the boundaries between generations. If an adult child resumed a more dependent status, the parent had to resume duties usually long since discarded. In fact, role confusions developed if a grandparent was forced into becoming a parent not only to the child but also to the grandchild.

When this shield of privacy was lowered, parents took actions that would seem interfering if a child's spouse were present. They also could become unwilling confidants to their children. New-found intimacy in the relationship also arose when daughters and mothers shared status characteristics. As on daughter commented, "Our relationship is better than ever, perhaps because we are both single." Another mother described her relationship with her son: "Now our relationship is better than ever. I told my son it was a shame it took a divorce to get us closer together." The usual distinctions between intergenerational roles can also become blurred for divorcing parents and their children. With increased loneliness and the need for emotional support, divorcing parents often turned to their children, who then became confidants and companions. Barriers between generations in regard to sexual privacy on occasion broke down, as cited earlier, and parents and children shared their romantic activities.

CONTACT AND RECIPROCITY

In regard to social contact and aid, both generations, on the whole, gave quite similar reports on the more straightforward facts about the parent-child relationship. The following findings on measures of social contact and services exchanged come from the reports of divorcing children rather than their parents. Thus, further breakdowns on the basis of gender differences in adapting to divorce can be observed. The following findings point to three overall conclusions, which characterize the manifest content of the parent-child relationship.

First, there were frequent interactions between generations, a finding in part due to our selection criterion of residential proximity between parents and their divorcing children (table 6.1). With parents and child residing in the Bay Area, they potentially were separated by, at most, an hour's car ride. While few parents and children shared households, almost half lived in the same neighborhood, here defined as walking distance or a short car ride. Another one-quarter lived within a thirty-minute car ride. Given this geographic propinquity, it is not surprising that we found frequent social contact between parents and children. Over one-third of the dyads saw each other either daily or several times a week, and another one-third got together at least weekly. Telephone calls were often exchanged daily.

Women tended to be in closer contact with their mothers than were men. Although this difference was not statistically significant, 70 percent of the women, in comparison to 55 percent of the men, were in at least weekly contact with their mothers. Women's mothers were also more active as grandmothers in the aid they extended after divorce. Men tended to rely on their par-

Table 6.1
Relationships between Parents and Divorcing Children
As Reported by Children
(by percentage)

	Male (N = 20)	Female (N = 32)	Total (N = 52)
Proximity to Parents			
Household/neighborhood	30	55	45
Same area (thirty minutes)	40	16	25
About an hour away	30	29	30
Contact			
Daily/several times a week	30	35	33
Weekly	25	35	31
Less than weekly	45	30	36
Reciprocity from grandparents			
Economic aid	85	70	74
Frequent babysitting/services	33	71	56
More contact with divorce	45	50	48
More services with divorce	60	60	60
Dependency relationship			
Adult child dependent on			
parent	47	33	39
Generations interdependent	16	17	16
Generations independent	37	50	45

ents more for economic aid than for services such as babysitting, while with women the reverse was true. In any case, most divorced men and women reported that contact with parents had either increased or stayed the same following their divorce. Where an increase in contact occurred, they associated it with the divorce. About 60 percent of the men and women reported their parents had increased their supports because of divorce-related needs.

Second, the instrumental aid parents gave to children and grandchildren also was impressive. Almost 75 percent of the parents gave some form of economic help, and 22 percent supplied regular income maintenance to a divorced child. Less tangible forms of support were also common. In 63 percent of the cases, vacations were taken jointly, usually with the parents picking up the tab. Invariably, holidays were celebrated together. Additionally, a majority of the adult children reported that they went to their parents for advice; most often children went to fathers with their economic or legal problems and to mothers for advice on childrearing.

Fathers often assumed a protective stance with their daughters, particularly in protecting their economic interests. They were vigilant during the divorce settlement to assure that there was an equitable division of property. In several cases, the maternal grandparents had provided the down payment for a house, which after some years was worth much money. With the no-fault divorce settlement and the equal distribution of assets, the house usually had to be sold and the proceeds divided. Problems arose, as illustrated by one grandfather who was challenging this occurrence in court. He told us defiantly, "I'll kill anyone who tries to take away the roof over my grandchildren's head."

Third, while reciprocity between generations was frequently extended, most aid was unidirectional from parents to adult children. Troll and Bengtson (1979) found the same pattern in their study. Three-quarters of the children received financial help from parents, but in only one case did a child contribute money to a parent. Over half of the grandmothers babysat, but only one-quarter of the children had helped a parent during an illness. Finally, in comparison to the countless favors parents extended in household chores and chauffeuring of grandchildren, children rarely performed such services for parents.

It is likely, then, that adult children are a potential reservoir of support for parents, but only if they have stabilized their own situation. In three cases the mothers needed help from their divorced daughters, and in each case the daughter responded with alacrity. The mothers' needs arose respectively from impairment from chronic illness, recent widowhood, and a recent divorce. None of the daughters, however, had small children or other competing commitments. Even if there were serious needs, the value placed on independence was prominent. For example, one mother, who was housebound and in a wheelchair with arthritis, still struggled to live independently. While her daughter did not offer full-time help, the daughter's efforts were appreciated. "Every Saturday she comes to help—cleans my cupboards and kitchen— very good about helping me. She mentioned moving in, but I don't think parents and children should live together." Her daughter remarked: "I might have to move in—she can't stay there much longer. It would drive her crazy though—she's as neat as a pin. When I don't see her, I feel guilty, and when I do, I resent being there. And she insists on living alone."

Changes in Organization over Time

By our last contact with these families, the dominant emphasis had changed for the majority of divorced individuals who had initially placed a high priority on their relationship with their parents (Johnson 1988c). In most of these cases, they had reasserted the primacy of the nuclear family once they no longer needed their parents' support. In the process, their lives had become less open to their parents' observations and comment. In their new status they intentionally distanced themselves from their parents: "When you go to your parents, you give them control over your life. They can comment on your life and make you uncomfortable if they disapprove." "I love them, but I've got to be my own person." "We can only become friends after I'm independent from my parents."

Contact with parents did not decline over time for the sample as a whole. Nevertheless, priorities were revised even when a close relationship was maintained. As the divorced children reassumed a more independent status, a new type of solidarity was forged that was not based upon their dependence. In some cases, this change occurred because of a child's remarriage; and in other cases, the parents themselves established more distance from their children. Of the seven divorced individuals who remained dependent upon their parents at Time 3, five did so out of economic necessity.

Most of those who chose the nuclear family option at Time 1 continued to preserve the privacy of this unit and maintain their distance from their parents at Time 3. Where conflicts with parents were present, these continued over time. Where the relationship was "friendly at a distance," that type of interaction also continued. Changes that resulted in a stronger generational bond at Time 3 occurred either because of financial difficulties of divorced individuals or because of the illness and dependency of parents or children.

Most of those who emphasized the amorphous networks continued this form of solidarity over time. They were friendly with former in-laws at the same time they accumulated new in-laws and friends through further marriages. They retained a friendly and casual relationship with parents, but one that emphasized expressive over instrumental functions. They also retained flexible and permissive values, as did others in their networks. Such flexibility most likely encouraged continual exposure to alternative life-styles that were incongruent with their parents' norms.

DEPENDENCE AND POWER RELATIONSHIPS

Many who turned to parents for help following the divorce became dependent upon them. Less than half of the divorced individuals were able to maintain their independence from their parents. More men than women were dependent on their mothers (see table 6.1). Economic assistance from mothers to sons was common; and in some cases, men needed their mothers to assist them when their children visited. Also, some men asked their mothers to function as intermediaries between themselves and their former wives in negotiating parental responsibilities.

Dependence often had beneficial effects, as suggested by indirect evidence. For example, divorcing parents who reported fewer problems with their children had mothers who were more involved. The mood of divorcing parents was also associated with their relationship with their parents. Morale was significantly higher when their relationship with their mothers was reported as satisfactory. In fact, 60 percent of the children said that their lives would be much harder if their parents were not in the area.

The structure of the relationship between a parent and adult child changes according to the needs of the situation. When the divorcing child becomes dependent upon his or her parent, a previously symmetrical and egalitarian relationship may become more hierarchical and asymmetrical (Emerson 1976). With increased status differences, parent and child become more emotionally and socially distant from each other. As hierarchies change, interactions also change. For example, one mother and son had a friendly, egalitarian relationship. Initially she told us, "He is my best friend—my favorite child." By our second contact, she had begun to resist the large financial sacrifices she was making to help her son save a failing business. After taking out a second mortgage on her house, she decided: "I have to get tough—I can't support his dreams anymore. I am forced to wield the financial axe." Understandably, the relationship became more hierarchical as she exercised more power. By our next contact, her son had given up his business venture and taken a well-paying job. He was also repaying his mother. She again described the relationship as a friendship, but, much to her dissatisfaction, one at a distance— "He is the one who breaks my heart. Now that he no longer needs me, I don't see him anymore. I guess he got tired of me telling him what to do."

When adult children no longer need help, status differences may diminish. Some respondents emphatically rejected norms of obligation and endorsed values of independence over dependence. As discussed in the next chapter, when children are dependent upon a parent following divorce, their situation is incongruent with societal norms. Negotiations take place between generations as their levels of power and dependency change. Because of the values placed on equality, there are oppositional and contradictory forces operating—the ideal of symmetry and egalitarianism and the reality of inequity and asymmetry. Power theorists propose that as ego becomes dependent, alter is granted power over him, a situation that is accentuated if ego has few alternatives to the relationship (Emerson 1976). Such situations were common in this sample. Many sons had to turn to parents for economic help. Daughters often called upon their parents to babysit or provide supplemental income. Since such situations were incongruent with the norms of independence and equality, tensions arose. To reduce these tensions, they denied their dependence or else found some means to rationalize it.

One woman was forced to return to her parents' home with her four-year-old daughter because she had many debts and insufficient income to pay rent on an apartment. Over the next eighteen months, she saved money and was finally able to move to her own place, much to her satisfaction. Even though she had a good relationship with her mother, she reported: "It took me so long to become independent, I hated to move back home. I do everything to retain control over my life, because you give people authority over your life once you ask for favors."

Thus, despite protestations of equality, the structure of these relationships fluctuated according to the degree of dependence of one generation upon another. When adult children became dependent, they found themselves in a position that erased any equality with parents they had achieved upon reaching maturity. Their parents could pull rank because they were giving far more to a child than was expected at such ages. Once the immediate problem was solved and an adult child could function without parental help, the structure returned to a more symmetrical one. The next chapter will illustrate these processes through case-study analysis.

SOURCES OF TENSIONS
BETWEEN GENERATIONS

Incongruent expectations were a major source of tension between generations among our respondents. Such tensions may be accentuated because our culture permits much normative flexibility in defining this relationship. Within limits, both generations have the freedom to determine patterns of interaction and reciprocity. The optional nature of the norms, however, should not obscure the reality that this system is regulated by very clearcut norms regarding personal freedom. Not surprisingly, then, in our sample, by far the strongest normative directive expressed by both generations was that adult children should not come back to the family after marriage. Since independence values so pervade relationships, grandparents maintain a stance of noninterference. In this study, rather than taking the initiative and seeking a more active role, their most important function in their children's families was, in their words, "to be there if they need me." They also strongly condemned "being judgmental," or taking a value stance regarding their children's lives. Such responses indicate a more passive role in which the initiative must come from the child.

Despite the flexibility permitted them, family members do not lose their status as parent or child. Few dissolve this most primary blood relationship. Instead they renegotiate it—usually when a child leaves home. Divorce provides another transition point at which negotiations take place and expectations are revised. The changing expectations of parents and children may not always be compatible, so failures in meeting each other's wishes can lead to conflict. If norms of obligation and reciprocity are revised by the child but not by the parent, problems can arise. For example, at least one-half of the adult children in our sample were dissatisfied with their mothers' responses to their needs. One overworked mother of young children turned to her parents for assistance in babysitting, but in her words, "I keep expecting something but there is nothing there." Her mother told us, "We have our conflicts over what she expects of me as a mother and grandmother. I refuse to give up my own life as she is asking me to do."

As described in the previous chapter, grandmothers were more concerned about what they should not do rather than about what they should do. Such a stance influenced the parent role. Mothers tended to wait to be asked to help. The norm of noninterference, while compatible with values on independence, was often so strong that needs went unmet in both generations despite the best of intentions. Such a stance naturally avoided conflict, but not surprisingly, it also created social distance. These differing expectations had other consequences as well.

The logical questions arising from this material are, what do children expect of their parents, and how congruent are these expectations with their parents' conceptions of their role? At the end of each interview, we asked a series of questions on hypothetical situations, such as "Should a grandmother get involved when? . . ." These situations were selected to discriminate between those that potentially involved extending instrumental versus expressive supports and those that distinguished between their children's and grandchildren's needs.

We observed prominent differences between generations in expectations of what parents should do. Adult children tended to want more help from parents with their emotional problems than parents felt it was appropriate to give. Parents, on the other hand, preferred involvement in more neutral areas such as occasionally babysitting, rather than intervening in their children's psychological or divorce-related problems. For example, in response to hypothetical problems, adult children were significantly more likely to agree that parents should intervene when a son was drinking too much, while parents preferred to leave that problem to professionals. Likewise, parents were less likely than their adult children to think a parent should get involved when a daughter was depressed. In responding to this question, the older generation generally concluded that there was little one could do in such situations, so the matter was best left to professionals. In marked contrast, children were likely to think a parent should become involved.

There was more agreement in other areas. Both generations tended to think that grandparents should not become involved in potentially conflict-laden situations with former in-laws, such as when a son-in-law falls behind on alimony payments or when he takes the grandchildren to his lover's house for the night. In regard to grandchildren, the divorcing parents were somewhat more likely to think their parents should not intervene on issues of supervision. While not statistically significant, these differences suggest that the younger generation wanted their parent to become more involved in the emotional domain, while they preferred that their parent not interfere in matters regarding the grandchildren or their relationship with their former spouse.

Children expressed ambivalence because they felt their efforts to enlist help from parents may have been rebuffed. Not surprisingly, if emotional succor was not always forthcoming, they felt hostile to their parents. Nevertheless, in situations in which the divorcing individuals needed a confidant with whom to discuss their emotional problems, they were very hesitant about turning to their parents. In response to the question, "Who would you go to when you feel down in the dumps?" only nine percent of the children chose a parent first, in comparison to 30 percent of the parents who would go to a child. These findings suggest that neither generation sought out the other as a confidant, a source of help that is important in reducing stress (Cohen and Syme 1985; Lowenthal and Haven 1968).

Thus, these reports reflect contradictory directives for the parent and child. Adult children wanted their parents' support in both expressive and instrumental functions, yet they did not want

parents to intrude in raising children. Nor did a child consider a
parent a confidant. In turn, parents tended to shy away from
helping with their child's emotional problems, yet they felt they
should passively "be there" if needed to see to a grandchild's needs.
Any action beyond that may be viewed as interference and hence as
a violation of their most cherished norms of independence. Grandparents were also fearful of having to take over tasks ordinarily
performed by parents because of the risk of losing their own freedom in the process.

Responses to other questions on who would be the first person
they would go to for help, indicate that economic support was the
most common type of help sought from the adjacent generation.
After a long recuperation from surgery, one-half of the sample
would seek help from the alternate generation. The percentage of
respondents who would turn to the alternate generation for help
was lower than one would expect given the high proportion who
actually did help each other. Such discrepancies may reflect the
ambivalence commonly found in the parent-child relationship, an
ambivalence that appears to be associated with conflicting tendencies: the need for emotional support and the need to be independent from each other.

The emotional climate of the relationship is one of oscillation
rather than equilibrium between approach and withdrawal, intimacy and distance, or neutrality and intensity in emotions. The
respondents also discussed the idea that one had to work hard to
regulate the emotional climate of the parent–adult child relationship. In fact, emotions were often depicted as having a finite
quality, so that if the other person demanded too much, one's
own emotional reserves would become depleted. As one daughter commented about her relationship with her mother: "Mother
is the type who would take all I have to give. I can't be so weak-
ened. I have to be careful that she doesn't relax and think I'll
always be there. She would want me with her every minute."

The nearly unilateral flow of material support from parents to
divorcing children was counterbalanced by an expectation of a flow

of emotional and social support in the reverse direction. Because that expectation was not often fulfilled, there was an undercurrent of tension discernible in the interviews with both generations. More directly, it was found that only one-fifth of the children and slightly fewer of the mothers described the parent-child relationship as free of conflict. Daughters tended to report more conflict than did sons, most likely because childrearing practices became a source of contention when grandparents were more involved in babysitting.

The most noticeable source of tension had to do with unmet expectations. Only slightly less than half of the children and even fewer of the parents reported that the other generation met their expectations. The remainder either complained about their needs not being met or they maintained that they had no expectations whatsoever. More of the children (80 percent) had some expectations of their mothers as grandmothers. These expectations were more likely to be met than were their expectations of their mothers as parents.

GENDER DIFFERENCES IN THE RELATIONSHIP WITH ONE'S MOTHER

While few significant gender differences were found in the level of contact and reciprocity between generations, in the emotional domain, differences were prominent. Daughters tended to report more ambivalent relationships with their mothers, and they were more likely to complain of lack of support: "I needed help and it didn't come. Now I resent this." Others described their mother as lacking in understanding and affection. Some complained about problems communicating at times when they attempted to restore closeness. In fact, women tended to worry more about their mother's approval, sometimes to the point of avoiding confidences—"I couldn't talk to her about my problems because I knew she'd disapprove." In all, there was a long list of complaints about the relationship and a very short list of its strong points. In fact, there were very few mothers and daughters who were in frequent contact yet still able to maintain a completely unproblematic relationship.

Although some sons complained that their mothers made too many demands upon them or treated them as youngsters, these men by and large reported improved relationships with their mothers following their divorce. They reported better communication with, more support from, and increased respect for their mothers as mothers and grandmothers. Several men described their relationship as more equal after the divorce, as their parents joined them in easing the strains on grandchildren affected by divorce.

There are several explanations for these gender differences. First, mothers of divorced sons potentially have a key role to perform—acting as intermediaries between their sons and their grandchildren. As noted above, paternal grandmothers often retained a relationship with a former daughter-in-law, and by doing so, they retained a link to the grandchildren. Some termed their house as "Command Central," through which the conflicts associated with marital breakdown could filter and be mediated by the paternal grandparents. In the process, some conflicts were moderated. In any case, mothers of sons always had less to say about their grandchildren because their sons were unlikely to be full-time parents. Sons also experienced less stress from being overburdened, so they made fewer demands on their parents and were consequently less likely to be disappointed if these demands went unmet.

Mothers and daughters have a far more complex relationship. Usually the relationship is more emotionally charged because it entails more activities, the sharing of confidences, and advice giving. Historically, daughters have spent more time around the house than sons and have shared domestic tasks with their mothers. The sharing of tasks not only keeps them in more intimate contact, but also provides more opportunities for conflict. In any case, the divorce usually brought mothers and daughters in this study even closer together because daughters were forced to turn to their parents for help in raising their children. In doing so, there were more opportunities for conflict and dissatisfaction in the relationship.

SUMMARY

The findings reported here reflect the subtleties and complexities of the parent-child relationship. Relationships are more difficult to analyze yet more interesting because of divorce-related changes. In most cases, parents and their divorcing children became more intimate when the parents provided support. In other cases, parents and children kept their distance from each other even when a child's or grandchild's needs were unmet. In those cases where large, flexible kinship networks formed, parents and children maintained a friendly relationship, but one that often did not meet social and emotional needs.

In keeping with the characteristics of family at this class level, most parents and children tried to maintain a compatible, egalitarian relationship and one in which they implicitly attempted to minimize hierarchical differences. Their preferred stance was a hands-off policy, and they tried to be nonjudgmental about each other's lives. These attempts were often frustrated during the divorce process, and tensions arose that undermined the quality of the relationship.

◇ 7 ◇

THE DEPENDENCE VERSUS INDEPENDENCE DILEMMA
with Peter Stromberg

W E heard endless variations on the importance of not being dependent, not being a burden, and not interfering in the lives of other family members. On this issue the generations were in resounding agreement. Despite the popular assumption that it is the children who are seeking autonomy while their parents are clinging to them or making demands on them, as often as not, the parents were as concerned about their own independence as were their children. They feared being forced into situations where they were dependent upon their children or in which their children and grandchildren infringed upon their own freedom. These findings are consistent with research in gerontology, which shows that older people prefer activities with age peers to interaction with children (Wood and Robertson 1978). Gerontological research also consistently finds that older people have higher life satisfaction when their networks are dominated by age peers (Blau 1973). Thus, we cannot think of parents being consciously excluded from their children's lives, but instead must think of a mutual agreement to respect each other's autonomy.

To review the issues discussed to this point, first, the theme of dependence versus independence occurred so frequently in discussions with respondents that I conclude these issues were the greatest source of tension between parents and adult children. In previous chapters, the nature of family attachments was traced to cultural factors and the position of these families in the mainstream, middle-class subculture where independence from the family is highly valued. Parents and children are expected to be intimate at a distance and to respect the privacy and autonomy of their nuclear family. While parents are expected to give material aid if needed, they are not supposed to infringe upon the privacy of a child's nuclear family. Cultural directives on the value of independence exert considerable pressure on individuals to avoid making demands on the adjacent generation (Clark 1969). As La Gaipa (1981) has observed, the expectations held by both generations are too idealized, overdemanding, and unrealistic and thus merely compound the problem.

Second, as is common in this subculture, there are few specific normative prescriptions regulating the relationship between parents and adult children. Thus, individuals are uncertain as to who should do what for whom in those situations in which one needs help. Incongruence between values and the objective needs of the situation can be analyzed using Merton and Barber's theory on sociological ambivalence (1963), a condition they relate to the incompatible normative expectations that are built into statuses and roles. In some cases, widely held values are not organized into a set of norms giving more specific directives. Ambivalence is also likely when contradictory and competing norms enter into social definitions of relationships (Coser 1974). When these norms are incongruent with objective demands impinging upon the relationship, some measure of ambivalence most likely will persist. Yet manifest rejection of the norm leaves emotional residuals—guilt, a sense of sin, pangs of conscience—which can create tension for the individual and ultimately affect the quality of the relationship.

Third, with marital changes, boundaries that had previously defined the objective and subjective distance among family members will change. Three types of boundaries change. Physically, the nuclear household affected by divorce dissolves. Socially, if a divorcing child must turn to a parent, expectations and role behaviors change. The structure also changes, with the parents usually having more power over their child. Also, the adult child's life becomes less private and more open to the parents. Psychologically, individuals redefine their relationship experientially as one means to reduce tension. Redefinition of their views and the meanings they had assigned to their relationship also blurs conceptions of generation boundaries, perceived levels of intimacy, and so on.

Before illustrating these dynamic processes through case studies, it is useful to place theories of dependence within the framework of our analysis of the families to date. To review the events within the divorce process, great emphasis has been placed upon the cultural setting. In comparison to the country as a whole, the Bay Area has a pronounced cultural emphasis on personal freedom and self-fulfillment. Such directives are often in conflict with the reality of situations when an adult child needs help. When tensions develop between parents and adult children in family systems where these contradictions arise, various strategies are employed in their negotiations with each other. One common mechanism is to redefine the relationship in such a manner that the meaning of the relationship changes for both partners in the dyad. Alternatively, these mechanisms may entail restructuring one's needs or seeking help elsewhere. Others may distance themselves so they are not placed in the position of providing or receiving assistance. Still others find some compromise situation in which they can tolerate the ambivalent situation.

In the following discussion I will refer to three overall types of dependency, which may occur on either a temporary or long-term basis. The first type is instrumental dependency, which includes relying on others for economic support and services. The second type, social dependency, concerns the reliance on others for sociability and to combat loneliness. The third type, emotional dependency, concerns the need to have others reaffirm one's self-concept, act as confidants, and provide for one's psychological well-being.

While research on generational relationships tends to measure "gaps" on the basis of political values and more objective factors, here I am primarily interested in values that more directly impinge on daily life—those that concern personal freedoms versus responsibilities. It is in these areas that any generation gap in values and life-style is likely to occur.

THE GENERATIONAL EMPHASIS

As the objective measures indicate, it is quite common for the ties between the divorcing individuals and their parents to become strengthened. The dominant unit of solidarity is the blood tie between generations. Strengthened solidarity between generations, however, is based upon the dependency of the adult child, a situation (as noted above) that is incongruent with our norms. Thus, ambivalence arises and produces tension in the relationship. Individuals have three types of options in dealing with an ambivalent parent–adult child relationship.

1. They can redefine the relationship in order to change the meaning of their ambivalence. For example, parent and child may "become friends" and blur status differences that have been a source of conflict. Others redefine the relationship in idealistic terms, choosing to ignore undercurrents of tension.

2. Other parents and adult children carry on their relationship in the face of considerable conflict and mutually agree to tolerate a conflictual and ambivalent relationship. Nevertheless, conflict occurs below the surface.

3. A third option is to redefine the dependency as normatively acceptable and an inevitable adjunct to the divorce process. Both generations accept it as serving the best interests of the adult children who have been affected by divorce.

Becoming Friends: A Redefinition of the Relationship

One technique commonly used to cope with such tensions was to emphasize those dimensions of the relationship that are commonly found in friendships. The ideal of friendship was often expressed by both generations. "I'm more of a friend than a parent." Or "My mother is my best friend." A friendship model as applied to the parent-child relationship implies minimal status differences, an emphasis on expressive functions, the sharing of confidences, and so on. These conceptions can be used as a means to disguise the dependency in the relationship. It is possible that such a disguise may reduce tension as divorcing individuals and their parents deal with the inevitable strains of the divorce process and the high needs of the adult child. Consistent with family processes discussed earlier, the boundaries between generations often become blurred with an adult child's divorce.

Parent-child relationships that were described as friendships occurred in 30 percent of the dyads. The most commonly shared characteristic of the grandmothers in these dyads was their marital status: two-thirds were widowed or divorced. Most of the others reported dissatisfaction with their marriages. The sex of the child was not a factor; these relationships were as likely to be found in mother-son dyads as in mother-daughter dyads. Finally, the grandmothers in these relationships tended to espouse more youthful age norms and egalitarian family relations. Most of the relationships described as friendships were fairly intimate and involved sharing many confidences, particularly in regard to their failed marriages. As a divorced daughter reported of her mother, "We have a unique relationship—we share all confidences, including our problems with men." Obviously the removal of a spouse in either generation removes a formidable competitor to the mother-child relationship. As one mother reported, "There is a sense of restored closeness now that the barrier [his former wife] is removed."

Divorces in both generations can act to minimize age differences and thereby equalize the relationship. In some cases, mothers and daughters formed coalitions against men. One mother in her seventies pointed to the similarities between her daughter and herself. "Both my daughter and I wanted a man we could respect. Neither of us found such a person." Another reported: "Both of us married young. We had to hold down ten jobs at once. We married lazy men—workwise and sexually." Her daughter agreed, "Our relationship gets better as we get older, maybe because we are in the same boat—we're more like friends now."

In one family, the guise of friendship between generations resulted in a coalition forming between a mother and her daughter that actually excluded an adult granddaughter who had recently divorced. All three generations were interviewed. All three women minimized age and cohort differences. They were proud that they were mistaken for sisters when they went out together. Beneath the surface, however, considerable tension had developed, despite the guise of friendship that all three generations espoused.

The grandmother, a very dominant woman, maintained a strong hold over her daughter, who had been quite depressed and ineffectual since her divorce. Because of that depression, much of her dependency on her mother was realistic. Yet this close bond, she found, prevented her from making friends or dating. Even when she was married, she told us, her mother competed with her husband for her attention. After the divorce, her mother had an open field. In the mother's words: "My daughter is my best friend. We talk every night about anything and everything. I'm her psychiatrist. We take vacations together. She's my favorite traveling companion."

Although this strong coalition appeared to ease the strain of divorce for the daughter, the granddaughter, also recently separated, felt excluded. "My grandmother is always there. I haven't been alone with my mother for three years. I feel emotionally deprived, and so are my children. I have no opportunity to get close to my mother." She went on to describe her mother's dependency in a maternal tone similar to that used by her grandmother: "Mother has so many emotional problems that I try to protect her from mine."

A more detailed case study illustrates the form of a parent-child relationship where the elements of friendship are emphasized. Susanna, a forty-year-old mother of three, had divorced her husband, she told us, to escape a traditional, stifling marriage.

Susanna reached this decision to leave her husband through psychotherapy and exposure to the women's movement. In her interview, she stressed her mother's role of confidante during the process. In contrast to her close relationship with her mother, she had always had an unsatisfactory relationship with her father, who died when she was in her late teens. He had been a strict and old-fashioned father, she reported, who imposed unrealistic rules upon both Susanna and her mother. Susanna assumed the role of her mother's protector from this authoritarian man. She summed up her relationship with her mother by saying, "I've always had mother in my back pocket. I've never really separated from her." Now she depended upon her for babysitting, occasional financial help, and, most importantly, emotional help.

Susanna's mother had a similar view of the relationship. First of all, she valued the emotional support she received from her daughter. For instance, she fell in love with a man who she later discovered was living with someone else. Being most upset, she discussed the matter with her daughter. The mother also received more practical help from her daughter—"For example, my mother died, and I need help to get rid of all her household stuff. She'll be the first to come and help me with that."

In this relationship one can observe a number of features typical of a close parent–adult child relationship that operates under the guise of friendship. In the first place, the parent is likely to be widowed or divorced, so parent and child share single status. Second, they are likely to emphasize expressive rather than instrumental functions. Although both women extended and received instrumental help, they repeatedly mentioned emotional exchanges as being central to the relationship.

Especially illuminating in this context was the manner in which money was exchanged. Susanna's mother in fact contributed significantly to Susanna's income, but such contributions were always disguised as gifts to avoid the implication that they were regular financial support. Thus, she chose to give money on holidays on which gift giving is common—Christmas and birthdays—and supplemented this with "unexpected" gifts at irregular intervals. For example, Susanna mentioned, "Last year, Mother gave me one thousand dollars out of the blue." The unexpected quality of the gift removed such assistance from the category of income support to that of an impulsive and generous act, a spontaneous expression of friendship.

Like friendships, this mother-daughter bond was seemingly symmetrical in status in contrast to the usual hierarchy of parents and children. Both Susanna and her mother minimized distinctions between their statuses and roles. In their emotional interchanges, the two women would speak freely with one another about the most intimate details of their lives. The attempt to equate the parent-child dyad with friendship is one means to resolve, or at least to disguise, the basic ambivalence described throughout this discussion. Friendship relationships are more symmetrical and more voluntary than parent-child relationships, and they are based more on mutual interests. These cultural ideals are in direct opposition to the realities of the parent–adult child relationship during stressful periods, which could account for the undercurrent of tension observed in many families. If, as is likely, adult children become dependent on a parent after a divorce, they are granting parents considerable power over them. While the parent might deny such influence, at the covert level it exists and must color the quality of the relationship. At the same time, parents usually feel they must fulfill their responsibilities even if they want to maintain their freedom from such responsibilities. One form of reconciling these contradictions is to relabel the relationship as a friendship and by definition remove obligation and dependency from direct social view.

Not surprisingly, most who initially chose this option established more distant relationships by our third contact. For example, Susanna and her mother both changed their lives considerably. Susanna had fallen in love, and while not yet married, she spent most of her time with her lover. Her mother had inherited money from an uncle and moved from a dark flat in the city to a bright, cheery condominium in the suburbs. She was dating and involved in many activities. She at last freed herself from her husband's relatives, who had continued to exert control over her, and she was seeing her grandchildren far less. She commented, "We both have our own things to do." Her daughter told us: "Mother's life is much fuller now. We don't see her as much, because it is not as convenient to visit. I think it is time for me to let go."

Carrying on Despite Conflict

Some parents and their adult children are actively involved with each other despite a high level of conflict. In this type of relationship, the fundamental ambivalence evident in most parent–adult child relationships is given free reign and is completely visible and tolerated by both parties. Of the seven dyads that were dominated by conflict, four were mother-son relationships. In most cases, the child was quite dependent economically and socially on the parent and thus was unable to establish enough distance to diffuse the conflict.

The relationship between Mary and her mother is a good example. Mary was under quite a bit of stress following her divorce because the care of her two-year-old son was preventing her from doing the travel necessary for advancement in her corporate career. Her mother agreed to take over the full-time care of her grandson, even though this decision entailed considerable sacrifice on the part of her and her husband. They had to delay moving to a retirement community in Southern California. One of the few things that Mary and her mother agreed upon, however, was that young children should not be raised by strangers.

According to Mary's mother, this was the first time since early childhood that Mary had explicitly asked for her parents' help. She had been an independent child who very early became absorbed in activities outside the home. "She became independent when she started to school—sounds impossible, but it is really true. She fell in love with school immediately and with the sports and other activities. She spent more and more time with these activities and less and less time at home. Even when away at college, she never once called to say she was homesick." Mary supported this assessment, saying she had been "mentally independent" from her parents since childhood.

The grandmother babysat every weekday and often on weekends, so that her grandchild spent substantially more time with her than with Mary. In fact, on some holidays, the grandparents would take their grandchild to their other daughter's house, while Mary spent the day with friends. The grandparents even went into counseling with their former son-in-law and his new wife to work out conflicts over custody, an action in which their daughter refused to participate.

Mary acknowledged her dependence on her parents, appreciative of the sacrifices they were making for her son. At the same time, she was very critical of them. She said that they were always too protective of her and too critical of her life-style. "They have always been so square. I hated living at home for as long as I can remember. I hated the fights about my behavior. They always set hours and tried to control me. My father was too moralistic. My mother was well-meaning but too nosy." When asked if her life would be different if her parents were not in the Bay Area, her ambivalence was noticeable. First she said, "If they weren't here, I wouldn't have to see how depressed my father is and how unfree my mother is." Then she quickly added, "But then—ugh—my kid would be raised by strangers. He would always be with someone who is not a relative."

Mary's mother regarded her daughter with ambivalence. "Mary is incredibly selfish. She only sees me now because she needs me. Once my grandson starts to school, I'll never see them." She also felt that her daughter devalued her. "I have to be careful what I say. She calls me a martyr. She has no respect for housewives— thinks our opinions are of no value. It's like our roles are reversed. She is the one who is constantly giving me advice—correcting my grammar or telling me how to lose weight. She is spoiled and not much fun to be with."

This case illustrates a compromise between the daughter's long-standing independence and her virtually total instrumental dependency upon her mother. The compromise was sustained by the willingness of both parties to carry on with a close relationship in the face of major conflicts. However much the mother and daughter complained, their complaints seemed to have no practical effect on the supports the grandmother provided.

In most of these relationships, the emotional climate fluctuated as both generations expressed feelings of love versus hostility or, at best, frustration. Emotionally charged relationships occurred between mothers and sons as well as between mothers and daughters. For example, a sixty-year-old widow concluded, "The secret is to never expect anything and then you won't be disappointed." She then went on to describe the polar conflicts between her need to be independent and her need as a parent to offer guidance to her son. "The best thing you can do for your children is to lead your own life. I will never be an appendage to my children's families." In reality, all of her children had come to her for money, housing, and help with education. "My son hasn't cut the cord yet. I see the shade come down over his eyes when he doesn't want to deal with things. I have to say things. He owes me so much money, so I have the right to pull rank." Her son, age thirty-four, also reported a mixed relationship. "I try to maintain a civil relationship. She meddles quite a bit but knows she can only go so far. She doesn't nag. That's on the surface. Beneath that, we have a complex relationship. There are many things I resent. Like she is always treating me like a child. And I feel guilty when I disappoint her."

In two cases, sons had defused the tension in their relationship with their mothers by becoming more intimate with their fathers and avoiding going to their mothers. For example, one young doctor, who lived next door to his parents, reported: "I have a better relationship with my father. I don't trust Mother—her emotionality gets me off balance." His mother described her relationship with her son: "He has a very gut emotional expressiveness. It's too much at times—so much so that we both pull back. Now we are good neighbors—we borrow cups of sugar. And I know when he wants to complain about something. He invites me over for coffee. Last time he had a long list of complaints for me."

In most of these interviews, expressions of love were frequent, just as were expressions of disappointment because of unmet expectations. In some cases, a genuine intimacy also pervaded the relationship despite high conflict. In others, the relationship would undoubtedly have become more distant had the child not been dependent on the parent. In those cases, the children were usually economically rather than emotionally dependent upon a parent.

The Perpetuation of Dependency

In some families, both parents and their adult children readily adapted to a child's dependency. In doing so, the power structure changed, and the parents usually exerted more control over their children's lives. Most parents in this sample, however, would never do so blatantly; instead they attempted to exert subtle and indirect influences over their child's behavior. The patterns of reciprocity in these dyads were also markedly asymmetrical, with the parent giving far more help to the child than they received in return.

Acceptance of dependency occurred with only eight parents and adult children. Five were males who had become economically dependent upon the parent. The remaining three were women who were dependent on the parent for both emotional and instrumental help. This small group can be further divided for analysis. First, there is a dependency arising out of the child's immaturity, which makes it necessary for the parent to step in to help. Second, there is the dependency arising out of necessity, where the grandparents' actions are essential if the grandchild is to remain within the family. Third, there is the culturally approved dependency often found in traditional families.

An example that conforms very well to the dependency arising from immaturity of the child is the case of Leslie, a forty-year-old mother of four children. Her husband had left her for another woman after fourteen years of marriage. Her husband was described as a perfectionist, and she did not live up to his standards. Leslie's parents were neither surprised nor chagrined at their daughter's divorce. Her father said that he had seen it coming and that his former son-in-law was a "cold fish" whom he was glad to be rid of.

Her husband had provided well for her during the marriage, and there remained evidence of an affluent life-style. Although having serious financial problems, she continued living in an expensive, architect-designed home. The home was luxurious though sparsely furnished because her husband had removed many possessions. Leslie was permitted to remain in the house until she could get her life in order despite mounting debts. Sitting there in a large, half-furnished living room with a vaulted ceiling, she was dressed in a cashmere sweater, designer slacks, and lots of gold jewelry. Leslie described her situation with nonchalance, although her financial situation was uncertain. She had not worked since the early years of her marriage. She had tried a sales job after the separation, but found it to be too demanding while raising her children. Her parents then decided to provide monthly income supplements so she could maintain her life-style.

With four children under the age of ten, Leslie was very dependent upon her parents. According to Leslie, they were extremely cooperative: "Let's put it this way. If I ask for something, they make every effort to accommodate." They babysat, drove the children here and there, contributed financially, took the children on vacations, and took them over weekends so that Leslie could date. Their financial help was substantial. In addition to income supplements, when Leslie needed money to tide her over until the sale of her house, her parents loaned it to her interest free. When Leslie was having trouble with her car, they gave her theirs. They seemed very solicitous and did not begrudge the substantial help they gave their daughter: "We sit back and see what to do to

make life easier for Leslie. We'd like her to get her life in order—
meet people and establish a normal social life."

In those areas in which they did not agree with Leslie, such as
in certain aspects of her childrearing philosophy, the parents were
careful not to interfere. Leslie's mother admitted that sometimes
her daughter's behavior vexed her, as when Leslie returned late
from skiing weekends without calling her, leaving her with grandchildren worried about why their mother had not returned. But
she did not mention these complaints to Leslie, nor did she
attempt to give her advice.

Leslie readily acknowledged her dependent relationship with her
parents: "I've never broken the umbilical cord. I've always lived
near them. Even when I was in college, I came home most weekends. I've never really been on my own." At the same time, neither Leslie nor her parents attempted to be friends or emotionally
dependent upon each other. In fact, Leslie reported a distant
relationship and one in which few confidences took place. "There
were never any mother-daughter talks about sex, marriage, or
whatever." This situation continued relatively unchanged throughout the course of the research. Undoubtedly, the relationship had
developed in this manner because of Leslie's immaturity and her
long-standing propensity to go to her parents when any problem
arose.

In other cases, a child's dependency stemmed from realistic
needs that made the parents' help vital. For example, one couple
prevented their grandchildren from being placed in foster homes
when both parents abandoned them. In another case, a divorcing
man could not care for his daughter when his former wife had a
mental breakdown. His parents flew to the East Coast to help.
Eventually they brought their young granddaughter home with
them and raised her for several years until their son remarried. One
young mother ran off to live in a commune, leaving a distraught
young husband who could not manage a six-month-old baby
without his mother's full-time surrogate mothering.

Another woman, age twenty-six, was abused by an alcoholic

husband and forced to return home with her infant son. She
eventually stabilized her life after a period of almost childlike
dependence on her parents. At the time of our last contact, she
was working, dating, and had placed her baby in a good day-care
center. Her mother reported that while they had taken every step
possible to assist her in reorganizing her life, they had little influence over her. "She is maturing and we just hope she'll be
self-sufficient some day. We're family and here to help each other."
According to her daughter's interpretation, her parents had done
so much for her, "I can't get along without them. I'd still be
married without their help. They are talking of moving South
with retirement. If they do, I'll have to go with them." Yet she
felt that her mother retained some distance from her: "There are
things I'd like to tell her about, like getting an abortion, but she
doesn't want to know about it. So I pretend I don't take their
advice, that I'm independent of them. But they have a lot of
influence over me—more than they realize."

These individuals extolled their parents for their help and
pointed to the power the parents had over them. The parents, on
the other hand, insisted that they wanted no repayment and, in
fact, were waiting for the child to become independent. One
grandmother, when asked what she expected of her son said,
"Nothing! I'd die first."

These reactions are quite different from those in the two families
that portrayed the dependency of traditionalism. In one case, the
son had just ended his third marriage. He and his two sisters, who
were divorced career women, went to their parents' house daily for
lunch and to watch the soaps. This pattern was encouraged by the
mother despite her disappointment over their many divorces. She
described her son, "I think he is a marvelous person, but there's
something wrong with him as a husband." Her son described his
parents as "my two best friends. We may disagree, but they've
always stood by me. I can go to them and I know they will always
be there." Usually in such families, religious values and family
obligations are stressed.

RELATIONSHIPS IN THE NUCLEATED
FAMILY SYSTEM

Those divorced individuals who attempted to maintain the privacy of their nuclear unit usually did so because of a problematic relationship with their parents. Some parents and divorcing children went through several stages in their relationship during the divorce process. Initially the divorce brought them closer together. Then, when the child placed demands on the parents, conflict developed and both parents and the adult child withdrew. In other cases, the relationship between adults and their parents had always been distant, and it did not change with the divorce. Few tensions arose because the possibility of a child's dependency did not arise. In those families, it was common to preserve the social distance in order to avoid dealing with controversial issues, a move sometimes referred to as establishing a demilitarized zone (Hagestad 1981).

Individuals with a distant relationship with parents were unlikely to turn to them unless in serious need. Such individuals usually viewed the relationship as optional. They maintained contact and reciprocity only intermittently and only when convenient for them. If they sought help on occasion, they distanced themselves again after the crisis passed. Very few parent-child relationships broke down completely; instead, tension was controlled by the mere fact that contact was only intermittent. When together, they carefully followed rules of etiquette, maintaining civility and avoiding emotionally sensitive discussions. Obviously, with this distance, conflict did not have many opportunities to surface.

Twenty-seven percent of the parent-child relationships studied could be described as civil but distant. In half of the cases, the children reported that anger and conflict had recently arisen; and, evidently by mutual agreement, these individuals had decreased contact and abandoned many activities they had previously shared. The other six of the twelve dyads had always had a distant and formal relationship, which could be characterized as "friendly disengagement."

Friendly at a Distance

John is a thirty-eight-year-old businessman, the oldest of five children in an affluent family. He was married in the late sixties and had three children. Several years ago he and his wife began to "grow in different directions," a development that seems to have been related to his wife's return to school to study art. Throughout most of his marriage, John lived near his parents but left it to his wife to manage their relationship with them. With his divorce, an already distant relationship with his parents became even more distant. He regarded his father as "dominating," and he was determined to conduct his life without advice or help from his family. "My mother thinks I'm ignoring them," he said, "and in a way I am."

John characterized his relationship to his parents as friendly, autonomous, and somewhat distant. When asked to speculate on the character of his life if his parents did not live nearby, John did so in a distinctively unengaged manner: "They are kind of a source of comfort and some strength, just knowing they're there. I've thought some about, gee, what happens if and when my parents die? Even though we're not real close, it's something I've thought about."

John's mother gave a similar picture of the relationship, saying that her son is "personable," even though they are not very close. She attributed this in part to her son's "uncommunicative" personality, and noted that he had always been independent of them. While she wanted her son to be happy and tried to be supportive, she realized she had little direct influence in his life: "I don't think what we say matters too much."

This somewhat distant relationship did not seem to trouble John's mother. She had limited expectations for her son—she only hoped she could "keep the doors open." She also emphasized independence. "There's nothing I call on him for, nor vice versa. We're close, but not like some families. . . . I don't ask anything of him or vice versa. That's the way I was brought up. My kids would resent advice or influence. I never say anything." With John's gradual disengagement from his family and the domination of his father, there were few opportunities for conflict to develop.

Conflictual at a Distance

There are other types of distancing mechanisms in the parent–adult child relationship other than the "friendly disengagement" of John and his parents. In more conflictual relationships, there is usually a great deal of incongruence between the parent's and child's reports, with the parent usually reporting a more positive relationship than the children do. For example, a seventy-one-year-old mother was very satisfied with her relationship with her forty-two-year-old son, a recently divorced man. "We seem to understand and agree on just about everything. We're close but not on top of each other all the time. I expect what I do get—love and consideration—but no obligations." The only reservations she expressed were indirect. "Way in the back of my mind, I had hoped for a closer relationship, but when I think about it, I know it just couldn't be."

In marked contrast, her son was seething with hostility. "I've had psychological problems since childhood and have been in therapy ever since. My mother and father are the source of my unhappiness—they are so unloving. They are always fighting. I have to mobilize myself to call them. They are really crummy people. I can't accept their values. I have to be free of them."

As mentioned above, in about half of the cases in this category, social distancing was not a recent development. These families had long preserved each other's privacy, avoided expressions of feelings, and strongly endorsed their independence from each other. In fact, some respondents concluded that maturity rested upon freedom from a parent. As one respondent put it, "I love my mother, but

I've told her I have to be my own person." A grandmother expressed the value of independence even more strongly: "Our family is just like this country. We keep our cotton-picking hands off of each other's lives. I was raised that way and I raised my son that way." In such cases, the situation was agreeable to both generations. One mother described her daughter as noncommunicative and said, "She has been that way since childhood—like I am— not an open person." The daughter agreed, "I'm like my mother —not an open person."

Another daughter reported a psychological distancing from her parents at an early age because her parents had been unable to meet her needs. "There's a lot of hurt and misunderstanding there. Since I was four years old I felt I couldn't get what I wanted. I always felt alone—that my mother didn't love or accept me. Later, by my teens, I put up a wall—and it is still there." Her mother merely reported: "At first, we were real close. Then she kinda drew away. Once she started working, I didn't see her much. She's trying hard to be independent, and we respect that."

The child's complaints of unmet needs were a continual source of ambivalence. A thirty-year-old woman described her relationship with her mother: "I've always tried desperately to be loved. I created a relationship with my mother whether she wanted one or not. Therapy made me see this more clearly. Mother likes people more if they are not sucking on her tit. I tell her I've been sucking for a long time and there is nothing there." Her mother, who lived one hour away, had little to say about the relationship except that they were independent of each other. Then she added: "It just occurred to me that I've never stayed in her house all night. That's odd, isn't it?"

Some of the children had been exposed to the self-actualization movement and in due course came to accept its principal tenets: one should be open, expressive, and unafraid of feelings. They wanted this type of relationship with their parents but knew that it would be difficult to establish. Yet they were still determined to add more affective content to their interactions. A forty-three-year-old man, a highly successful professional, told us with some regret: "Mother has called me for advice once—about a car problem—never about anything important. Touching and kissing were never part of our relationship. It's very formal. I'm trying to develop a different relationship with my sons." His mother merely reported: "We are independent. We don't go running to each other with our problems. I only tell my son about a problem after it is solved." Another reported a similar view: "Mother is too proper and distant. I'd never confide in her."

These examples of distant relationships, whether conflictual or harmonious, show that such relationships usually cover over barely suppressed anger about unmet emotional needs, most often on the part of the children. Some children were angry and frustrated at their mothers for not providing them with the emotional support and interdependence they viewed as the key ingredients to happiness. Their parents, on the other hand, typify the American character so frequently described in our historical literature: a self-reliant, independent type whose strength rests upon autonomy from entanglements.

From time to time, we presented our interviews to clinicians, who analyzed the more psychodynamic processes going on in relationships between parents and their adult children. Relevant here is the observation by one clinician that the divorcing individuals with a distant relationship with their parents were expressing an emotional hunger to restore the love and security of childhood. It can also be pointed out again that in more objective measures of these children's expectations of their parents, they were more likely to want a parent to become more involved with their emotional needs than in fact the parents felt it appropriate to be.

PARENTS AND CHILDREN IN
INDIVIDUAL-CENTERED NETWORKS

In the following chapter, the characteristics of those who form amorphous networks of divorce and remarriage chains will be reported in detail. At the risk of repetition, it should be noted here that parents and children who participate actively in these divorce and remarriage chains have less contact and exchanges of reciprocity with each other than do those who more strongly emphasize the generational bond. Perhaps these diverse relationships become substitutes for the intergenerational bond. Individuals may participate in such networks because they do not have compatible and rewarding relationships with their immediate family. Generally the ideology of individuals in these networks is dominated by norms of independence and autonomy. They usually insist upon the freedom to form and dissolve relationships, and they often reject norms of obligation between parents and children.

In families with these large networks of friends and relatives by blood or marriage, the sheer number of people and the flexible nature of relationships act to defuse any tensions that form between parents and children. Relationships in such families are usually voluntary and based upon personal preferences. Without any norms of obligation or responsibility, individuals can leave a relationship that is too troublesome.

Usually both generations in these families take steps to prevent any dependency on each other. The relationship is not all-consuming but rather "friendly at a distance." One son, who had custody of two teenage daughters, reported of his mother: "We've worked out a good relationship. We know each other's limits." He went on to express some dissatisfaction with his mother; he said he had encouraged her to become more involved with his daughters than she was willing to become. "I really need her help with female advice to my daughters. I make innuendos, but she doesn't seem to be so inclined."

Another grandmother explicitly attempted to keep a sociable

but aloof relationship with her son. "It's a mellow relationship—not a lot of contact. There are social visits but no advice
given. He was very supportive of me when I divorced, and I try to
return it. Also, I feel he loves me and would like me to love him.
I don't expect a thing from him—just that he be kind to me."
Her son agreed, "We have a distant but loving relationship."

Strong values of independence also come through in these
descriptions of more distant friendships. One mother equated her
friendship with her daughter with independence: "My daughter
and I have always been good friends. We share everything that
might come up. We talk everything over. We help each other in
any way we can." Then, in the next breath she said, "We've
always been independent of each other." Throughout these discussions then, there is an underlying theme: independence is the basis
for a successful relationship. This independence means, above all,
that the parties will not place too many demands on each other:
"We've worked out a good relationship, but we don't test it."

Mrs. Gilmour is a sixty-year-old grandmother who had four
children in her first marriage. When the children were in their late
teens, their father died. After raising them alone, she remarried at
age fifty. Her four children were living nearby along with their
families, as were her current husband's mother and his adult
children. Since two of her children had been married and divorced
twice, her network was large and complex, particularly because
she maintained friendly relationships with two of her former
daughters-in-law.

Her son, Bill, who also was part of our study, was living about
thirty minutes away. She usually talked to him several times a
month and saw him monthly. They had a fluctuating relationship
but one in which tension rarely came to the surface because they
did not see each other often. She explained: "I have nothing to say
about his life and he doesn't want to hear about my problems. We
both are busy—we don't spend much time with each other. But I
don't have to see him to let him know how much I love him."

Then she went on to illustrate how her relationships were

complicated by her own remarriage and the acquisition of a complex social network that required juggling the step and biological
relatives. "I am tired of trying to fit my children in with my
husband's children. I am at a stage of life when parents should be
separate from their children. I feel my children should be totally
on their own. Like my son is his own person even though I gave
birth to him." When she listed those whom she considered family,
she included two of her four former daughters-in-law along with
her own children. The family group had optional ties, as she
indicated, "I've shelved any expectations I have for any of them,
and I hope they have done the same."

Her son confirmed the intermittent tension in the relationship.
"I love her, but it is easy to get upset with her. We just step back
from her—my children are fond of her but don't see her much."
By our second contact, he reported that his relationship with his
mother was much better. "In the past three years, we've had our
ups and downs, but now I am more understanding of her. I think
it is because I am older." Along with this new maturity came his
informal role as marriage counselor to his mother and her current
husband. In other words, the relationship had shed many elements
of the conventional parent-child dyad and taken on new functions.

This family is only one example of relationships in complex
kinship systems; others will be discussed in the next chapter. This
example does illustrate the changeable nature of relationships in
these networks and the intermittent kinds of support that can be
expected from them. Relations between parents and their adult
children are potentially diffuse, for there is a propensity to let
specific situations determine interactions rather than to rely on
long-standing norms and expectations. In the absence of established norms, relatives of blood, marriage, and previous marriages
may be equated, and in the process, tensions between parent and
child are likely to be defused.

AMBIVALENT RELATIONSHIPS

In this analysis, we have depicted the parent–adult child relationship as potentially having an undercurrent of tension and ambivalence, which we have traced to contradictory and often inconsistent expectations on the appropriate degree of attachment and interdependence the relationship should have. In fact, a realistic dependency of an adult child arising from the post-divorce situation is incongruent with the cultural mandates of the Bay Area population, which so strongly endorses autonomy and independence. Because of the incongruence, expectations often go unmet—a situation that usually increases conflicts between generations. Despite these problems, however, little overt conflict is observed in the majority of the cases.

The means individuals use to resolve tensions are likely to be associated with previous patterns of interactions between them. In the post-divorce reorganization process, patterns of solidarity emerge that share a constellation of characteristics. If the intergenerational bond has always been emphasized, the relationship between parents and their children following a divorce may become strengthened. Such relationships can take several forms. Where tensions develop because parents and adult children make demands on each other, they can moderate these tensions by emphasizing the characteristics of friendship; that is, they can minimize status differences and stress social and emotional rather than instrumental interchanges. In other cases, parents and children can maintain their ties in the face of considerable conflict, usually because the high needs of grandchildren require contact and reciprocity. In a few cases, parents and children establish ties in which dependency needs are satisfied in a manner similar to traditional family systems.

Where parents and children have always maintained distance from each other, this pattern usually continues after the divorce. Neither has expectations for the other, nor do they go to each other for help. They maintain private lives in which they exclude each other even though many prefer a closer and more supportive relationship. In sharp contrast to both these patterns is the parent-child relationship in individual-centered networks. Here the relationship between parent and child is usually compatible because any emotional intensity is diffused by the sheer numbers and complexity of their social world. Although parents and children are not necessarily supportive of each other, they usually have a reservoir of friends and relatives they can call upon. Since former and present in-laws are often equated with blood relatives, these ties may compete with the bond between generations. These patterns will be further analyzed in the next chapter.

KINSHIP AFFILIATIONS AND INTERGENERATIONAL RELATIONS

In many intact families, the relationship between a parent and a married child becomes triangular, with the child-in-law exerting considerable influence. Such influence does not always end with divorce, so any understanding of intergenerational relations also entails the study of in-law relationships. For example, Mrs. Gilmour, who was discussed in the previous chapter, has a full and complicated life and is surrounded by a large extended family. Unlike in the traditional family of the past, however, these relatives have accumulated as a result of the numerous marriages, divorces, and remarriages of herself and her children. In eliciting information on her kinship system, we found a proliferation of in-laws who stay in active contact with each other.

Mrs. Gilmour was most articulate in describing her complex life: "Unlike death, which is final, the problems of divorce go on and on. You can never lose in-laws even if you want to." Her relationships with her sons and their children varied a great deal because of her diverse relationships with their former wives. First, her eldest son, Kevin, was married briefly during college, and when that marriage ended, her contact with the former daughter-in-law also ended. His second marriage was to a woman, Anita, who became Mrs. Gilmour's friend. The two women shared many interests, and both wanted to continue the friendship after the divorce. Mrs. Gilmour also continued to be active with the grandchildren of this marriage, she explained, largely because of her friendship with their mother. At the time of this interview, Mrs. Gilmour was seeing more of Anita than she did of her own son, even though both lived nearby. She always asked her son first for holiday dinners; if he could not come, Anita joined them. At the time of the third interview with Mrs. Gilmour, she and Kevin rarely saw each other. They had always had an ambivalent relationship, but these conflicts had never impeded his mother's relationship with the mother of his children.

Her younger son, Bill, had also been divorced twice, and his second ex-wife remained Mrs. Gilmour's close friend. She and her fiancé were invited to holiday dinners if Bill could not attend. At the time of the third interview, Bill was engaged to a woman whose parents were acquaintances of the Gilmours, so they had begun to socialize frequently. Mrs. Gilmour's relationship with Betty, Bill's first wife and the mother of her grandchildren, had been so conflictual that they maintained no contact. In her view, Betty had undermined Bill's second marriage by constantly referring to his second wife as "that whore," especially in conversations with her children. The children's subsequent lack of respect for their stepmother, she felt, caused problems in Bill's marriage. Even though Bill had joint custody and his children spent three days a week with him, Mrs. Gilmour saw them no more than once a month. It had been hard, she concluded, to maintain relationships with Bill's children because of her conflicts with their mother. "I also have to be very careful of what I say, so they won't know what I really feel about their mother."

She also used subjective notions of distance to justify her rare contact with Bill's children. She evaluated contact on an annual basis even though she potentially could see them on a weekly basis. The distance involved between them was less than one hour by car even when the grandchildren were with their mother. Mrs. Gilmour contended, however, "I don't see them because of the joint custody. Since they spend half the year with their mother, I only have half a year to see them." Her son reported to us his dissatisfaction with his mother's lack of involvement, so it appears that he imposed no barriers to her seeing her grandchildren as much as she wanted.

Mrs. Gilmour had several ideologies on family life that are relevant to understanding these kinship forms. For instance, she emphasized the emotional aspects of relationships. "I'm very involved with my children and grandchildren. If they hurt, I hurt. If they are happy, I'm happy." Nevertheless, she defined membership in her family according to whom she likes. In reviewing her relationships with her grandchildren, she said, "My family is whomever I like, though I have gradations of love and liking. Some children are easier to love than others. Ronnie is the love of my life. I feel she is a special part of my life. Jerry I love, but totally differently. Johnny is hard to love. He keeps his distance. Jimmy is an easy child to love but too rambunctious. . . ."

Mrs. Gilmour also complained that her large and active family was too complicated in several respects. For example, she commended her son for maintaining an active interest in his children and scrupulously observing joint custody. She concluded, however, that it was hard on her grandchildren. "If both the mother and father play active, committed roles as parents, it is hard for the children. They are loved and wanted in two households and must go back and forth. Their loyalties are tested." She also found this complication in her own remarriage; she had had some problems balancing demands between her children and stepchildren and their families. "I've come to the sage knowledge that people who remarry have to make laws beforehand about their own families. No matter how I try, I can't make my husband's children like mine. It causes emotional dismemberment—it always pops up. Even adult children create an enormous strain in a second marriage. It should never be 'our family' but his kids and my kids."

Virtually everywhere there are inherent tensions created by marital changes. With marriage there is a rearrangement of households and redirection of loyalties and priorities. In many societies, tensions can arise when individuals must transfer loyalties from their family of origin to new spouses and their families. Frequently, in-laws occupy ambiguous positions, which are only clarified by formal social mechanisms. For example, most kinship systems cross-culturally are organized so as to avoid or lessen tensions. In unilineal descent systems, loyalties are officially shifted for one partner upon marriage. Where it is impossible to avoid conflictual in-law relationships, joking about relationships is common (Radcliffe-Brown 1952). Mother-in-law jokes in our culture are one rendition of the use of joking to defuse tensions between some relatives. In our society, a married couple establishes a new residence separated from kin; thus, much tension also is reduced by greater physical distance.

CHARACTERISTICS OF THE AMERICAN KINSHIP SYSTEM

The complex permutations taking place with divorce and marriage are congruent with the dominant configuration of the American kinship system—at least as illustrated by the middle-class families studied here (Furstenberg 1981; Schneider 1965; Schneider 1968; Schneider and Homans 1955). In the words of David Schneider, there are "no formal, clear, categorical limits to the domain of kinship" (1965, 289). Thus, the system has no effective rules defining the limits or boundaries of any kinship system. Such an open system permits the individual to make decisions about forming or dissolving relationships rather than following established rules. In fact, when Americans attempt to describe their relatives, the further out the relationships are traced, the more there is a "fade-out" or "fuzziness" in identifying who are kin (Schneider 1965). Individuals most often use subjective notions of closeness and distance rather than genealogical distance to identify their relatives.

In addition, while there are numerous types of classification, our system comprises two major units: the nuclear family and an amorphous group called kindred. On the basis of survey research, family sociologists conceptualize the kinship system as the "modified extended family" or the "kin family network," which is a loosely connected series of nuclear households made up of a person's families of orientation, or of one's birth, and procreation, or of marriage (Sussman and Burchinal 1962). The nuclear family is a residential unit structurally separated from the larger kinship unit.

Finally, the American kinship system is bilateral, meaning that the relatives of both husband and wife should be of equal importance. In reality, however, women play the key role in orchestrating kin affairs (Yanigasako 1977). Women have been described as the "kinkeepers," the primary catalysts for interaction and the primary links between relatives (Troll, Miller, and Atchley 1979). Nevertheless, each spouse forms relationships with the other's family of orientation and their relatives, but there are no expectations that these two sets of relatives must form relationships with each other (Wordick 1973). Thus, the opportunity for conflict between the two kin groups is minimized.

Because of the inherent elasticity in the system and its fuzzy boundaries, however, there are no barriers to expansion with marital changes. Multiple marriages enlarge the pool of potential relatives (Furstenberg 1981). Since the kinship system has no rules of closure, there are opportunities for diverse alternatives. For the child, there might be an advantage in acquiring a larger pool of parents, siblings, and grandparents. Kin ties are discretionary and without obligatory rules, so individuals can initiate relationships as their needs arise. One can predict, however, that the kinship system potentially can expand if the individuals choose to retain relationships with former in-laws at the same time they add in-laws with remarriage.

Divorce is more common in this loosely structured bilateral system than in corporate lineal kinship systems (Cohen 1971; Gluckman 1951). Marriage is the weakest link in any social structure, but it can be particularly unstable in societies, such as ours, where marriages are formed on the basis of emotional bonds independent of directives from the families of either partner. Although most kinship systems provide a safety net in the event of divorce; with its autonomy, the American nuclear family does not necessarily provide such security. As Bohannon (1971) concludes, divorce creates social problems only in those societies in which the household is based upon the husband-wife relationship. Since the males in our kinship system, in comparison to those in corporate kinship systems, do not have strong institutional pressures to perform family roles, their role can become peripheral after divorce.

TYPES OF KINSHIP REORGANIZATION

In the United States, approximately half of all marriages will end in divorce and 80 percent of the divorced individuals will remarry. Therefore, changes in kinship systems potentially are widespread (Weed 1979). Divorce and remarriage entail major changes in inheritance rules, redistribution of wealth, and extension of the incest taboo, as well as more subtle changes in relationships. One common result of divorce and remarriage, as illustrated by the Gilmours, is a more complex kinship system. If a marriage has produced children, the relationships do not necessarily end with divorce. Relatives by marriage may no longer be legally related after a divorce, but these individuals still share a blood linkage to the children. In our analysis of the wider extended family, we found that in almost half the sample an adult child's divorce and remarriage tended to expand the grandparents' kinship system because of the blood linkage. There are two potential groups: *relatives of divorce*, which includes former in-laws and their relatives, and *relatives of remarriage* and their relatives. Expansion of the kinship network comes from the marital changes of grandparents as well as those of their children. These relatives occupy positions along divorce and remarriage chains (Bohannon 1971; Furstenberg 1981; Schneider 1965).

Since we have no vocabulary in our language to refer to kin relations in situations of divorce and remarriage, we were forced to spend considerable time during the interviews clarifying the relationships. In one of the few studies of affinal relationships in American kinship, Schneider and Cottrell (1975) found that 75 percent of all contact with kin was with relatives by marriage, which attests to their importance. In the families under study here, divorce created additional categories of kin with whom contact was maintained. They included affinal relatives of blood relatives (my brother's wife) and the blood relatives of affinal relatives (my husband's sister).

To use the grandparents as a point of reference, the kinship system can expand in four ways: (1) relationships with a divorced child's former in-laws are retained, while new in-laws are added with a child's remarriage; (2) a former child-in-law with whom one has remained in contact remarries; (3) the divorces and remarriages of multiple children create several subsets of in-laws; and (4) remarriages of the grandparents following divorce or widowhood add another set of step and in-law relations. Obviously, divorcing individuals have an even more complex system than the grandparents, for their children may have membership in several households and kinship systems. The children in divorcing families often are the links between present and former in-laws.

In describing their kinship systems, most respondents began at the basic conceptions of "blood" or "marriage," consanguineal or affinal relatives, respectively (Schneider 1968). Then, informants expanded their definitions of kin to include the affinal relatives of consanguineal relatives (my brother's wife) and the consanguineal relatives of affinal relatives (my husband's sister). Clearcut definitions of in-laws, however, become murky when these relationships legally end with divorce. Although in-laws were never related by blood and they are no longer related by law, some of these relatives are related by a shared biological linkage to the children of the dissolved marriage.

Using a grandparent as ego, the following illustrates how the definitions of these relationships may influence whether they persist after divorce.

1. When a former child-in-law is identified by the affinal linkage, the relationship is defined as having ended with divorce: "My daughter in-law" becomes "my former daughter-in-law"; "my son's wife" becomes "my son's ex-wife."

2. When a former child-in-law is defined by a shared biological relationship, both symbolically and operationally, the relationship is more likely to be defined as persisting after the divorce: "My grand-children's mother remains their mother."

3. When the relationship with a child-in-law is defined as a friendship, the relationship is defined as continuing on that basis alone.

It is logical to assume that when the recognition of the blood tie is the basis of the definition of the family and kinship system, this recognition is usually extended to those with whom ego shares a blood linkage. Our flexible system permits individuals to decide how to define their in-laws. When filling in kinship charts, however, respondents commonly noted that they did not know where to place their in-laws. After a divorce, it is particularly difficult to categorize these relatives unless one recognizes the shared biological linkage, even when ties of affection have also formed. If the marital link rather than the blood tie is recognized in those kinship systems with frequent divorce and remarriage, there are interesting ramifications. If a son's wife is viewed as a daughter-in-law rather than the mother of one's grandchildren, the relationship is more likely to end with divorce.

A third option is available. Grandmothers who do not recognize the maintenance of the blood tie yet wish to maintain their relationship with a child's former spouse can identify that individual as "my friend." This definition has entirely different implications; it implies the relationship is voluntary, symmetrical, and without high expectations (Paine 1974). Such a definition can be contrasted to those based upon a shared biological linkage, which are likely to invoke some of the institutionalized expectations found in kinship systems.

Respondents frequently faced dilemmas in defining their

relationships with these individuals. For example, one grand-mother invited a former daughter-in-law to a wedding anniversary party. After some thought on how to identify her on her name card, she decided to recognize the blood tie rather than their friendship by identifying her as "relative" instead of "friend." It is likely that this relationship is durable and inclusive of both expressive and instrumental functions, for a grandson's mother, rather than a son's ex-wife or a friend, is likely to share the grandmother's interest in their biological heirs.

In our second contact with the grandmothers, we used a kinship chart constructed from information collected at the first interview to map the relationships grandparents and their children had with each category of relatives. These findings formed the basis of the typology of the families. First, those who dropped former affinal linkages after divorce inevitably had contracting relationships with in-laws. Usually these families fit into our first model of reorganization, one in which the parent-child relationship, or blood tie, was strengthened after divorce. Second, another group was nucleated in form, isolated from both parents and relatives. In many of these families, individuals remarried and replaced relatives of divorce with new relatives of remarriage, thus replicating the original kinship structure. Usually these families resembled our nucleated model of reorganization in their emphasis on the privacy and autonomy of the nuclear family. The third group retained former affinal linkages at the same time they accumulated new relatives by remarriage, thus expanding the kinship systems through divorce and remarriage. These families fit our third model of reorganization: individuals take advantage of the freedom the system permits in order to mold their kinship network to suit their own preferences.

Contraction with Divorce

The predictable kinship reorganization following divorce has a consanguineal emphasis (Johnson and Barer 1987). This pattern was found in almost half the families at the time of the first interview. For example, the Joneses have a divorced daughter. After the divorce, they severed the relationship with their former son-in-law and his parents except when specific occasions demanded that they meet (for example, the high school graduation of a grandchild). Their contacts with their former son-in-law's parents were confined to these special occasions and the exchange of Christmas cards. No holidays or children's birthdays were celebrated together. On occasion, they met their former son-in-law when he stopped by to pick up the grandchildren. The relationship was formal and distant, with each side attempting to avoid conflict. In families such as these, the in-laws are no longer considered relatives following divorce, nor are they considered friends. They are usually referred to as "my former daughter-in-law" or "my son's ex-wife."

In previous chapters, numerous examples were included to illustrate how parents and children form a strengthened bond following divorce. The parents in these families usually approved of the divorce and blamed the former in-law as the source of their child's problem. Thus, they found it difficult to maintain friendly relationships with former in-laws. Individuals in both generations espoused more traditional values, which perhaps explains why there was less marital instability in their wider kinship networks. Thus, their relationships were also more stable and unchangeable.

Replacement with Remarriage

In a common pattern of kinship reorganization, former in-laws of a child's divorce are replaced with new in-laws of his or her remarriage. Grandparents cease contact with the former in-laws and form relationships with new in-laws and steprelatives. Furstenberg and Spanier (1984) correctly point out that the repudiation of a former spouse strengthens the solidarity of one's new marital relationship. This same stance undoubtedly holds for one's parents. If they sever the relationships with relatives of divorce, it facilitates the accumulation of relatives of remarriage. Because of the strong ties often found between grandmothers and former daughters-in-law, however, the severing of ties is not automatic. Grandparents who had a friendly relationship with a former daughter-in-law often resist dissolving the relationship after their son's remarriage, even if their son pressures them to transfer their loyalties.

The transfer of loyalties from previous relatives, who were lost with the divorce, to new in-laws acquired through remarriage replicates the previous kinship structure. Earlier I concluded that the pressures for remarriage were strongest among those who emphasized the privacy and autonomy of the nuclear household. In such instances, individuals have more distant relationships with parents and other relatives. Of course, if the new partner has been married previously and brings children into the marriage, the privacy of the new unit will never equal that of the original marriage. Children in remarried families maintain biological ties in the households of both their mothers and fathers. If they are in proximity, the sheer presence of steprelatives and in-laws is a potential source of expansion. In coordinating graduations, children's weddings, and, most commonly, visitations with noncustodial parents, divorce and remarriage chains operate at least intermittently.

Expanding Divorce and Remarriage Networks

Kinship systems that expand with marital changes usually do so because of the recognition of the shared biological tie to the children of the dissolved marriage. Given the blurred definitions of in-laws in the kinship system in general, they also can be defined as friends. In any case, these systems can become quite complex because the former in-laws of divorce are retained while new relatives of remarriage are added. Often the criteria on who is to be included are similar to those of friendship—relationships are based on personal preferences or "everyone I like." While remarried parents may distinguish between a child and a stepchild, for example, they have a propensity to treat relatives of blood, marriage, and divorce on an equal basis in allocating affections.

It is also important to note that when kinship expansion occurs, it usually does so on the basis of female rather than male linkages. Grandmothers do not have a direct linkage to their grandchildren, for their children and children-in-law usually mediate between them (Johnson 1983a; Johnson 1985a). Divorce complicates this situation. A child-in-law no longer is legally a relative, yet that individual shares with the grandparents a biological relationship with the issue of the marriage. Since custody is usually granted to the mother, the paternal grandparents have a particularly ambiguous status.

The normative flexibility and the matrilateral bias of the kinship system are important in determining the nature of kinship relationships following divorce. Grandparents are not required to sever the in-law relationships of their child's previous marriage. Grandmothers can retain their role as "kin-keepers," those who initiate and negotiate activities among kin, with former children-in-law. In fact, as the following indicates, paternal grandmothers often remain friendly with a former daughter-in-law and in the process represent the best interests of the grandchildren. One can also suggest that the usual tensions found between mothers-in-law and children-in-law may dissipate after divorce if those tensions had centered on conflicts over a man's loyalties to his wife versus his mother. With the divorce, such a division of loyalties usually disappears (Sweetser 1964). It is interesting that grandmothers often refer to relationships with former daughters-in-law as friendships, and under this label, the relationship serves some practical purpose. It may compensate for a son's deficiencies as a parent and provide linkage to the grandchildren (Johnson and Barer 1987).

Retention through Coalitions with In-laws. Expansion by the retention of in-law relationships is particularly common among paternal grandmothers. For example, the Smiths are paternal grandparents who had always had a close relationship with their son's wife, Ann. Mrs. Smith, who had no daughters, took her under her wing upon her son's marriage. Having grown up in a poor rural family, Ann was socialized by her mother-in-law over the years into the Smiths' upper-middle-class, suburban life-style. The Smiths were very upset by the divorce but saw no reason to end their relationship with Ann. Their son remarried and moved to another suburb, a forty-five-minute drive away. He was swept up in parenting activities because his stepchildren were much younger than his own college-age children. His relationship with his parents continued to be friendly, but he was unable to provide a linkage between his parents and his children. He did not participate in holiday celebrations with his parents; they always celebrated with Ann and her children. To avoid the loss of the grandchildren and to continue a close friendship, the grandparents formed a parentlike relationship with their former daughter-in-law to the exclusion of their own son.

The grandchildren also had a reconstituted kinship system comprising their father, his new wife, and her children by a former marriage. However, this affiliation was less stable than the three-generation unit because their loyalties to their mother were reinforced by their father's parents. When money was given by the grandparents to the grandchildren, as was frequently the case, it was transmitted through Ann rather than their own son. Channeling aid through an ex-daughter-in-law obviously further strengthened the in-law coalition.

The Smiths' role was only achieved by forming a coalition with their former daughter-in-law. During the divorce process, their home was the meeting place for their son, daughter-in-law, and grandchildren. They were the mediators of conflict and the vehicles through which information was exchanged. In fact, their home was described as "command central" by their son. He also reported that his parents provided the common bond, or the linkage, between himself, his children, and his former wife. He felt that as long as his parents continued to perform this function, his bond with his children would continue.

The grandmother reported that her involvement had been facilitated by her long friendship with her daughter-in-law. "We've always been friends. Now the only difference is we don't talk about my son." Thus, after the divorce the personal options the system permits allowed the relationship to persist without the connecting biological linkage. Such coalitions between paternal grandmothers and their daughters-in-law can also compensate for a son's deficiencies as a parent. Some grandmothers were angry at their sons for failing as fathers. Those sons were less likely to provide them with linkages to the grandchildren. In fact, some coalitions grandmothers had with former children-in-law excluded their own children. One fifty-seven-year-old grandmother was extremely critical of her thirty-two-year-old son for ending an eight-year marriage. At that time, he also had made a career change, leaving a middle-class position, and had started an affair with a nineteen-year-old woman. Divorce ensued, and in the paternal grandmother's view, her six-year-old granddaughter was left "fatherless." She felt she had to step in and compensate for her son's deficiencies. It should be noted that in this family and several others, both sets of grandparents formed coalitions with one of the divorcing parents and worked together to support the grandchildren. From the point of view of a grandchild, the advantages of this arrangement are apparent, for the effects of divorce and the loss of a parent are moderated by the solidarity of grandparents.

Other sons, who could not always provide their parents access to their children, had such conflictual relations with their wives that they themselves were denied access to their own children. Whether blameless or deficient as parents, sons often resented having to share their parents' attention with their ex-spouses. Some sons accused their parents of disloyalty, and feelings of rivalry with a former wife arose on occasion. Other men wished to have no reminder of their unhappiness in the marriage and objected to their parents' disregard for their feelings. Eventually these men pulled away from parents or were further excluded from kinship activities.

Expansion by Divorce and Remarriage of Multiple Siblings. As an example of further expansive affinal linkages, after the divorce of both a son and daughter, Mrs. McCurn, a widowed grandmother, maintained an active relationship with her former daughter-in-law, who was currently living with her former son-in-law. She viewed this family unit as her most important one. Because both grand-children of divorce were now in the same household, the affinal linkage was strengthened. She also maintained friendly relation-ships with the mothers of her former children-in-law.

Mrs. McCurn also had a secondary unit comprising her son and his family of remarriage—his wife, her parents, and her child by a former marriage. Her divorced daughter had been married twice, and both times stepchildren were present. Since these children were in the vicinity, Mrs. McCurn also had some contact with them, and both her consanguineal grandchildren and her step-grandchildren called her "Nannie." A new grandchild was expected out of the union of her former children-in-law, and Mrs. McCurn would not speculate whether she would consider this child as equivalent to her grandchildren. Nevertheless, the birth of the child will increase this third-generation pool. This kinship system also illustrates how grandparents' kinship relationships can expand with multiple divorces and remarriages of multiple children.

This example portrays how elastic the American family and kinship systems are. Mrs. McCurn was taking advantage of the many options the system permits. Her relationship with her former daughter-in-law dates back to her son's high school romance, so she had come to regard her as a daughter. In contrast, the history of Mrs. McCurn's relationship with her own daughter was filled with conflict. She disapproved of her daughter's three marriages and promiscuous life-style and sided with the daughter's third husband after that marriage dissolved. Since she also was friendly with her son's former wife, she approved of their sharing the same household and felt it was the best family arrangement. They assisted her with household repairs, and they shared meals at least weekly.

In the ordering of Mrs. McCurn's family priorities, the in-law relationships competed with consanguineal bonds. Her son lived about an hour away rather than in the same community like his former wife, so contact with him was less frequent. Moreover, her son objected to this close bond between his mother and his former wife, one from which he felt excluded. For example, he refused to come to holiday dinners because his ex-wife would be there with his former brother-in-law. His mother insisted that he be more broad-minded, for she wanted all parents of her grandchildren with her, irrespective of their marital status. She was critical of him for not seeing his son as often as permitted in the divorce settlement. He was critical of his mother's hesitancy to form a similar close relationship with his new wife. By our third contact, he had only rare contact with his mother and his children, essentially having transferred his commitment to stepchildren.

Two-Generation Divorce and Remarriage Chains. Other systems can become even more complex. The Millers illustrate the most expansive kinship system found to date, although conceivably even more people could be added with additional divorces and remarriages. The system expanded at two levels through the divorces and remarriages of both the grandparents and their son. The grandparents divorced about the same time as their son divorced. In fact, Mrs. Miller and Alice, her daughter-in-law, became confidantes as they both were going through the stressful experience of divorce. With their remarriages, both grandparents added stepchildren and stepgrandchildren. While their son remarried and moved outside the area, their former daughter-in-law remarried and settled within a short car ride of both grandparents' residences. Mrs. Miller approved of her former daughter-in-law's new husband, concluding he was providing a more stable family environment than her own son had.

Through their contacts with the grandchildren, the Millers and their new spouses maintained friendly relations with Alice and her new husband. Both Mrs. Miller and her ex-husband's new wife babysat for the grandchildren, and both helped financially through occasional gifts of money. The grandparents were also acquainted with Alice's husband's ex-wife and his children and saw them occasionally when seeing their own grandchildren. Since the children of divorce and remarriage lived within a few blocks of each other, contact among stepsiblings was frequent.

In the third generation (G3), a viable stepsibling group formed, which added to the complexity of the system—particularly from the point of view of the grandchildren (Johnson, Schmidt, and Klee 1988). Complications arose, however, in such a kinship system as this one. Three members of the third generation and one member of the second generation had the same first name. Since the unit was a new one, no nicknames have been selected to discriminate between them. Thus, each one was referred to by both first and last name, even by a parent and sibling. Other problems had developed by our final contact with this kinship group. Although the children continued to move freely between the two households, territoriality had begun to develop over the allocation of bedrooms. Other problems arose from the sheer size of this third-generation unit, and a detailed specification of rules on what forms relationships should take became necessary. Instead, the ad hoc governance used led to some confusion, as illustrated by the failure to allocate physical space to each child.

KINSHIP REORGANIZATION AND
FAMILY ROLES

As these case studies illustrate, the grandmothers are linked to in-law relationships through their grandchildren, who retain biological ties to the families of remarriage of both parents. As grandchildren retain and accumulate relationships, there can be a cumulative effect on those grandparents who maintain close ties with their grandchildren. These grandparents can form relationships with their grandchildren's new stepparent and stepsiblings and, in some cases, their stepgrandparents. It is also conceivable that the grandparents will form relationships with a grandchild's new stepparent's former spouse and his or her relatives if they participate in activities with their grandchildren and their stepsiblings.

Grandparents in Expanding Systems

In determining the impact these expanding kinship systems had upon the roles of grandparents, we found four significant factors. First, expanding systems were much more common among paternal grandmothers, a finding also reported on a midwestern sample of grandmothers (Ahrons and Bowman 1982). In our sample, about one-third of the paternal grandmothers maintained at least weekly contact with former daughters-in-law, while only 9 percent of the maternal grandmothers had weekly or more contact with former sons-in-law (Time 1). This female linkage persisted even when a former daughter-in-law was no longer considered a relative. Since custody was most often granted to women, maintaining a relationship with the custodial parent provided a grandmother with a linkage to grandchildren that her own son could not always provide.

Second, the grandmothers in expanding systems were far less likely themselves to be in a long-term marriage. They were significantly more likely to be divorced, widowed, or in their second or third marriage. This finding is the only statistically significant sociodemographic variable associated with the expanded kinship systems. It is possible that the grandmothers who had also experienced marital instability had more flexible definitions of their family and relatives and had more permissive values, which they undoubtedly transmitted to their children. Endorsement of such values may have facilitated their children's serial marriages.

Third, other characteristics of the grandmothers in expanding kinship systems suggest modern women who adjust easily to multiple marriages. For one thing, these grandmothers were in less frequent contact with their children. They reported they had less influence over them. Most of these women also reported that they had no emotional reaction to the divorce and avoided assigning blame to either their child or their child-in-law. In fact, they were likely to view divorce as an acceptable means to resolve marital conflict. In other words, these women usually did not overtly disapprove of their children's often permissive life-styles. In contrast, the grandmothers in kinship systems that contracted following the divorce tended to subscribe to more traditional values (Johnson 1985a; Johnson and Barer 1987).

Fourth, the grandmothers in the expanding kinship system were generally more satisfied with their relationships with their children and grandchildren even though the relationships were not described as close. They were less likely to complain about the help they were giving to grandchildren, perhaps because they were extending less instrumental help. In comparison to the grand-mothers in the contracting systems, they exchanged less aid with their divorcing children. The grandmothers were less likely to report they had increased their support to a divorcing child, and they were less likely to say they would call upon a child if they were in need of help. These findings suggest that relationships in expanding systems may concentrate on the social and expressive functions. As such, they are more rewarding because the more onerous instrumental functions have been dropped.

Divorcing Parents in Expanding Systems

The responses of the divorcing adult children in these expanding kinship systems were consistent with most of the findings from the grandparents' interviews. They reported a more distant relationship with their parents. They were less likely to depend upon their parents for help than those in other types of organizations, and their parents were less likely to meet their emotional needs. While they reported fewer emotional problems themselves, they did report more problems in their children's adjustments than did those parents who had other forms of organization. Approximately one-third of the men and one-fourth of the women had expanding kinship systems after their divorce.

More individuals in these expanding networks had remarried. Like their mothers, these individuals also were at the modern end of the continuum in their values. They had more flexible definitions of family and relatives and were less likely to disapprove of sexual permissiveness. Many maintained compatible relationships with former in-laws, even to the point of attending their wedding celebrations or, in one case, participating in the delivery of a former wife's new child. Obviously these individuals also maintained friendly relationships with a former spouse's new spouse or lover. In such instances, divorce was usually a mutual decision and initiated in keeping with the values of the new freedoms. As mentioned above, these individuals also were in less contact with their parents and received less help from them.

CONCLUSIONS

As these findings illustrate, the most common relationship retained after the divorce of a child is that between a paternal grandmother and her former daughter-in-law. Thus, the female-linked or matrilateral bias so commonly found in American kinship groups is replicated here, but takes a form in which grandparents extend their kinship group to include not only relatives of blood and marriage but also individuals who are no longer legally relatives. Since an individual who is no longer the wife of a son remains the mother of one's grandchildren, one can personally define her as a relative. It is possible, then, that definitions and meanings assigned to kinship relationships are changing, and in the process, distinctions between consanguineal and affinal relatives may be more blurred today.

Indefinite boundaries make the kinship system operate more flexibly, permitting individuals considerable freedom to determine the form and the content of their kin relations. Given the values that are common in this sample, the new freedoms they endorse result in relationships between parents and adult children that are regulated by two norms—for the grandparents, the norm of noninterference, and for the children, the norm of independence. Such a kinship system also permits the formation of coalitions that circumvent or deemphasize the consanguineal ties. That the expansive tendencies often come through coalitions between paternal grandparents and their former daughters-in-law is consistent with the female-centered bias of the American kinship system (Yanigasaki 1977). The persistence of the relationship between paternal grandmothers and their former daughters-in-law serves several functions: grandparents retain a linkage to the grandchildren; they can function as mediators for the divorcing couple; and they often buttress the support network of the post-divorce family.

It is unlikely that expansive kinship networks would have occurred in a more traditional and rule-bound kinship system. Given the flexible rules of the American kinship system, it is not surprising that many individuals have accepted these freedoms and constructed a kinship system that permits them to emphasize affinal relatives of current and previous marriages. This emphasis is often at the expense of consanguineal ties. The freedom to form and dissolve relationships at will within the kinship system takes place in a cultural environment in which personal freedom and independence are strongly endorsed by both generations.

Such flexibility also is evident in conceptions of the family. Since loyalties and allegiances can be easily transferred without sanctions in the wake of divorce and remarriage, the biological or even marital linkage may become less significant during divorce and remarriage processes. Individuals then can construct kinship systems based upon their own preferences, the needs of others, and their own needs at any given time. Because the system is voluntary and rests upon changeable factors, however, it is uncertain whether the system is sufficiently stable to provide for dependent members. It is likely that relationships in these expansive kinship networks are more specialized in emotional functions and are less capable of meeting the needs of individuals in any generation. If so, these relationships are possibly more rewarding but overall less supportive.

◇ 9 ◇

CONCLUSION

DIVORCE creates a dynamic series of events which have an impact not only on members of the dissolving household but also upon the extended family and the relationships between generations. In this book I have reported the results of a study of the events surrounding marital changes, which was undertaken in hopes of learning more about the effects of divorce on the contemporary family. Divorce is viewed here as a vehicle for social change rather than as a source of social problems, and one that may have both positive and negative valences. Initially I assumed that the impact of divorce and remarriage would be particularly apparent in those families in which members were granted freedom to shape their family life to suit their personal wishes. The research site, the suburbs of the San Francisco Bay Area, is a prominent example of a subculture that encourages sexual freedom, self-realization, and independence from obligatory family ties. Not surprisingly, intergenerational relationships in this study are quite different than in those families with more traditional views on family life.

These cultural patterns have wider implications for future family forms, for it is apparent that new definitions are emerging on what constitutes a family, who should be categorized as being related to each other, and what kinds of expectations one should have of these relationships. There is some tendency today to bemoan the new freedoms or to take an alarmist view of the future of the family. In the popular media, for example, one commonly finds conclusions like the following review of the changing parent-child relationship in fiction: "In the '80s, connecting links between generations are loosening and the family is replaced by the self-obsessed individual" (Lenz 1987). The work of contemporary novelists may suggest such a conclusion. However, almost four years of study of modern, or avant-garde, families in a subculture noted for its modernism suggests no such simple conclusions can be drawn about relationships between parents and their adult children.

RECENT FAMILY CHANGES

During the 1950s, the marriage rate rose, the age at which people married decreased, the divorce rate dropped, and family size increased. This period was known as one of high familism. The nuclear family was viewed as the core unit; and in the ensuing years, the marital relationship, its origin in dating and courtship, and the levels of adjustment and the satisfaction occupied a large portion of the efforts of family researchers. Often called the companionate family, this unit specialized in emotional functions, while instrumental family functions were met by other institutions. Childrearing during this Spockian era (after Benjamin Spock) was considered enlightened as parents concentrated on psychological techniques to instill conformity in their children. The nuclear family was thought to be relatively isolated from the kinship system, so with a few exceptions, little attention was paid to the relationships married adults had with their parents.

In the various social movements of the sixties, the nuclear family bore the brunt of much social criticism. It was viewed as oppressive to women and as inhibiting self-actualization. Enlightened individuals suggested that such a family form frustrates the individual's need for attachment and community (Slater 1970). Since then, all sorts of innovative living arrangements have been devised. Although the majority of individuals have continued to live in nuclear families, the high rates of divorce and remarriage have engendered far-reaching changes in relationships within these families. With frequent marital changes, family structure and organization have changed both qualitatively and quantitatively.

Other cultural trends have accompanied marital changes in the family. First, the American character is itself changing. Although a character type can rarely be verified, the concept itself has fascinated social scientists and intellectual historians for years because many formulations are congruent with their intuitions. Most observers would agree that the well-known character types originally described by David Reisman (1952) no longer accurately describe most Americans. Neither the *inner-directed person* of an earlier historical era nor the *other-directed person* of the postwar era can explain what we have observed in the past two decades. Although there are numerous labels for this phenomenon, I have used Ralph Turner's (1978) term *impulse-directed* to describe the new American character type. Impulse-directed individuals are guided by their personal desires and preferences rather than by social conventions or normative directives. Turner's term has been useful in understanding many actions of the respondents in this research—the obsessive search for happiness and all the panaceas found in the self-actualization movements.

It is not surprising that impulse-directed individuals, those who continually search for the good life, feel ambivalent about their interpersonal relationships. Individuals want to be free to pursue their own interests, yet they want to have meaningful relationships with others—relationships that will bring happiness and permit the fullest personal development. The respondents' absorption in finding self-fulfillment in a relationship with a significant other is not unique to this subculture. In fact, research on the American family is dominated by the study of intimate relationships. In leafing through the *Journal of Marriage and the Family* in the past two decades, one finds a disproportionate number of articles on dating, courtship, and marital satisfaction and relatively few articles on children and parenting. Only recently have perceptive observers suggested that researchers are deemphasizing the key biological function of family—that of raising young children—

and placing too much emphasis on changing intimate relationships (Cherlin 1983; Rossi 1977).

In a climate in which personal freedoms are valued, cultural directives pose few barriers to divorce or to any nonconventional post-divorce arrangements. It was from such an American subculture that we selected divorcing families, all of whom had at least one grandparent living in the area. In the subsequent years, we followed their lives and studied how, in the process of family reorganization, intergenerational relationships were redefined.

DIVORCE AND ITS AFTERMATH

In subcultures such as the one studied here, there are few sanctions against divorce. Since self-fulfillment is expected to be found in a marital relationship, heavy demands are placed on a spouse. Spouses are often held responsible for their partners' happiness and contentment. When they fail in that responsibility, the marriage often fails. Because divorce is common, however, there is a large pool of eligible replacements; for many, the process of divorce is the process of replacing one spouse with another.

The situation in most families is dynamic, with divorce and remarriage common occurrences. Thus, for a social scientist, the divorce process is interesting to study, for the organization of the family is continually breaking down and subsequently reforming. In the process, divorce creates uncertainties because there are few rules or directives on how to behave. Individuals are able to construct new roles, to redefine relationships, and, on the whole, to restructure their lives. Such restructuring affects not only those in the nuclear household, but also others related to them. Relationships with grandparents and other relatives are also redefined and reorganized. The relationships between grandparents and their divorcing children are particularly interesting in such a subculture, for the children often must assume positions at odds with their parents' values. While independence from parents is extolled, some form of dependency may be necessary. I have suggested that such discongruence was one source of the ambivalence so many respondents expressed in regard to the intergenerational relationships in their families.

Some divorces appeared to occur without clear intentions because of the permissive environment in which the respondents lived. At the stage of marital breakdown and the preparation for the dissolution of the household, grandparents were not usually involved. The exceptions were those families in which intergenerational relationships were close and interdependent. Grandmothers in such families usually knew about their child's marital problems, approved of the divorce, and blamed the former child-in-law. In the majority of the cases, however, the grandmother kept her distance and avoided involvement until her child actually separated.

A second repercussion of divorce has to do with the boundaries distinguishing differences between generations and the roles of grandparent, parent, and child. Mechanisms that had established distance between parents and adult children changed. Boundaries that had protected the privacy of households often loosened. The expectations built into family roles and relationships also were revised, resulting in a blurring of the distinctions between generations. For example, adult children often became more dependent upon their parents or used their own young children as companions and confidants. Young children, in turn, sometimes became more mature in the face of their parents' distractions.

When the barriers were lowered after the departure of a spouse, many respondents turned to their parents, and in the process, their lives became less private. Adult children usually had to take the initiative in seeking help from their parents, however, for parents generally maintained a noninterfering stance. Such a stance suggests that the strong nucleated family emphasis is difficult to transcend in our society, and the strong endorsement of norms of noninterference remains throughout the divorce process. In any case, parents were ambivalent about an adult child's new dependency even when it was only a temporary phenomenon.

There is no doubt that ending a marriage creates much upheaval for the individuals involved. Nevertheless, the inexorable processes of reorganization continue to establish some equilibrium in most individuals' lives, although often interrupted again by further marital changes. Most respondents not only had their parents in the area but also had extensive networks of friends, self-help groups, and community organizations to ease the typical strains of divorce. And most individuals were quite adept at mobilizing such supports. There were few cases in which serious problems occurred, perhaps because all of these families had grand-parents in the area.

THE ROLE OF GRANDPARENTS

This research activity, which began as a study of grandparents, was expanded far beyond this concern. There is no doubt that most of the grandmothers were quite responsive to the needs of their children and grandchildren, particularly the younger women with young grandchildren. Nevertheless, virtually no grandmother in the sample wanted her role to resemble that of the traditional grandmother, a type they associated with old age and domesticity. Instead of being the grandmother of the past—a kindly, maternal, gray-haired woman—most wanted to be friends and companions to grandchildren.

They were particularly ambivalent about having to act as parents to their grandchildren, meaning having to discipline them and be responsible for their day-to-day instrumental care. Their conceptions of the preferred role were quite uniform—that of a fun-loving, youngish woman who rejects any hint that grandpar-enting is an old-age activity. In the process, they had abandoned their role of transmitting values typical of more conventional family life. Most women made clear distinctions between grand-parenting and parenting and concluded they could not perform the functions of both roles at the same time.

While conceptions of grandparenting were quite uniform, their actions varied according to their age. Those women who more actively responded were younger, they worked, they were married, and in all, they had an active life. After age differences were accounted for, differences in grandparenting essentially devolved upon the relationships they had with their children. These ranged from close and interdependent relationships to relationships in which expressive functions were emphasized to relationships that were distant and formal.

The grandparent role in large part is determined by the parents of their grandchildren, so most grandparents were relatively passive in initiating action unless asked to do so. Their status was particularly ambiguous because one parent of their grandchildren was no longer legally related to them. In any case, grandparenting is so critically related to parenting and to relationships with children and children-in-law that those relationships have been the primary concern in this book.

REORGANIZATION OF INTERGENERATIONAL RELATIONSHIPS

The grandmothers interviewed rarely viewed their relationship with their divorced child with the sentimentality they bestowed upon their role of grandparent. In fact, the parent-child relationship was characterized by underlying tension, which I likened to social ambivalence. I concluded that with the unscheduled life event of divorce, transitions in the relationships between divorced individuals and their parents were often regressive because a child reassumed a dependent status. Members of both generations had to revise their expectations of the other, and members of the older generation found themselves in a situation of having to give more of themselves to a child than they had expected to do at their stage of life. They were often forced into a parenting role, and this greater involvement provided more opportunity to observe and comment on their adult child's life.

Given this unanticipated regression in the relationship, it was not surprising to find tension and conflict. Even so, there was extensive contact between generations, which did not decrease over time. Although grandparenting activities declined, relationships with their adult children changed very little over time. Nevertheless, there appeared to be incongruity in their expectations. Adult children were more likely to feel that parents should be available to help them with their emotional problems than their parents felt was appropriate. Divorcing children did not want their parents to interfere in childrearing or offer unsolicited advice, while their parents felt they could voice their concerns.

As in most social science research, there was much variation in the actions of the respondents, although a large majority were quite contemporary in their endorsement of modern values on personal freedom and self-fulfillment. In the analysis of intergenerational relations, these families were categorized by the type of solidarity they formed after the divorce. During the process of reorganization, the ordering of relationships was fast-paced as the nuclear family dissolved and one of two parents departed. As the family was reconstituted and, in many cases, remarriage occurred, the relationships between generations also became dynamic.

With systematic longitudinal comparisons on the basis of these types of reorganization, it was possible to understand changes in intergenerational relationships. Where the relationships between generations were emphasized at our first contact, the divorcing child turned to a parent for help and assumed a status of relative dependency. While the relationships between generations became strengthened and the needs of the divorcing children were usually met by their parents, such a status was usually temporary. Most importantly, neither parents nor children wanted to continue relationships that somewhat replicated an earlier stage of life. In contrast, those divorcing children who stayed relatively distant from parents and attempted to maintain their abbreviated nuclear household without help from others were somewhat vulnerable and exposed to more stress. They had to perform the roles of two parents, often with diminished social and economic resources. Nevertheless, the post-divorce family structure did not change markedly in form except for the absence of one parent. Since remarriage was more likely to occur with this type of reorganization, however, the previous form was replicated relatively soon.

In contrast, some respondents formed amorphous networks in which friends and relatives of blood and of various divorces and remarriages chose their associations on the basis of personal attraction. Their lives were quite complex, for they had to balance opposing interests among their many relationships within a social context that mandated personal freedoms over normative strictures. Generally, these individuals constructed their own rules for managing multiple relationships rather than relying on conventional values. In fact, their values extolled the new freedoms: self-fulfillment, sexual freedom, and the priorities of egocentric interests.

It is this form of reorganization that is most interesting in any analysis of family changes, for individuals create networks of relationships that have the potential to fulfill needs ordinarily filled by relatives of blood or marriage. New criteria may be emerging for defining boundaries of the family based on personal attraction rather than ties of blood and marriage. Consequently, it is useful to examine the relative costs and rewards of this form of organization.

TENSIONS AND THEIR RESOLUTION

Those who emphasize the relationship between generations must deal with tensions somewhat differently than others, for with their interdependent intergenerational tie, more opportunity for conflict arises. Understandably, fewer tensions occur in relationships where the nuclear household takes precedence over the generational bond, at least if this priority is preferred by both generations. Contact is less, and neither generation has many expectations for the other. Those in the divorce and remarriage networks also have fewer tensions, if these arrangements are mutually agreed upon, because expressive functions are emphasized over instrumental ones. Generally, such individuals are more satisfied with their relationships, although these relationships are less supportive.

Variations in the reorganization of intergenerational relationships following divorce suggest, on the one hand, that an adult child's dependent status potentially creates conflict, even though the needs of the divorced and their children are met. To deal with conflict when a relationship is unlikely to be broken off, members of both generations often redefine their relationship by equating it with friendship. In "becoming friends," they are attempting to regard the relationship as more symmetrical and voluntary and more specialized in social and emotional functions. Such attempts are made to disguise dependency and the regression it often entails. On the other hand, other parents and their children retain a strong bond, yet they carry on in the face of considerable conflict. Although they agree to disagree, they do so out of necessity because the situation requires that they interact to meet the needs of grandchildren. In still other dyads, parents and their children accept the dependency on the assumption that it is a temporary situation.

In contrast, parents and adult children who place an emphasis on the nucleated family system can continue as before or even increase the distance between the grandparent and parent generations. Usually they have few expectations of each other, and both are satisfied with "intimacy at a distance." These dyads can be contrasted to those parents and children who participate in the changeable network of divorce and remarriage chains. While individuals in these networks report higher satisfaction with the parent-child relationship than do others, they also report fewer supports from network members than do those who rely on their immediate family.

Irrespective of their values and life-style, families in this subculture, like those in more traditional social contexts, have a latent reserve of family solidarity and supportive resources, which can be activated when needed. One such occasion is that of divorce, when grandparents respond to the needs of children and grandchildren. Another is a time of late-life dependency, when children respond to the needs of their parents (Johnson 1983b; Johnson and Catalano 1983). Unlike families in more traditional subcultures, however, both parents and adult children in this subculture have difficulty tolerating any long-term dependency of the other that may require self-sacrifice. Moreover, the norm of noninterference generally remains, so individuals are often uncertain as to what to do for each other. One common response is to tiptoe around trouble areas, feeling some responsibility yet hesitant to become intimately involved. In any case, there is an undercurrent of tension in these relationships, which is addressed quite differently than is the case in more traditional subcultures.

One tension-reducing mechanism stems from the freedom the system permits. Rejection of obligatory ties between generations means individuals are free to help and free to withdraw from the relationship at will. The freedom to choose what one does and to shape the form of the extended family can function as a buffer to control tensions that develop during times when support is extended. After crises are past, parents and adult children withdraw and establish more distance from each other. Thus, conflict is controlled in a way that enhances the quality of intergenerational relationships.

A second means to control tension lies in the straining toward egalitarianism in the families studied here. To create more symmetrical relationships, individuals often describe their relationships with their parents and children as friendships. As friends, parents and children reduce status differences between themselves and introduce an optional quality to the relationship. Nevertheless, as friends, they can expect more rewards than they would have in more traditional settings, where the burden of obligation may hang heavily on family members (Johnson 1978).

Finally, with such freedom to shape one's family, individuals, particularly in complex networks, are continually exposed to new ideas, which further activate family changes. With serial marriages of numerous individuals, new life-styles, values, and ways of conducting family relationships are introduced by the continuing accumulation of relatives. Relationships are more rewarding, if less supportive, when definitions of family transcend the bonds of blood and marriage to include those bound together by ties of affection. If both parents and children have networks in which they are free to define their family system to meet their own needs, then intergenerational relationships do not necessarily deteriorate. They may continue to function in an altered form.

REFERENCES

Adams, B. 1971. "Isolation, Function and Beyond." In *A Decade of Family Research and Action,* ed. C. Broderick. Minneapolis: National Council of Family Relations.

Adams, R. 1960. "The Nature of the Family." In *Essays in the Science of Culture,* ed. G. Dole and R. Carneiro. New York: Crowell.

Ahrons, C. 1980. "Crises in Family Transitions." *Family Relations* 29:533–540.

Ahrons, C., and Bowman, M. 1982. "Changes in Family Relations following Divorce of Adult Children: Grandmothers' Perceptions." *Journal of Divorce* 5:49–68.

Ahrons, C., and Rodgers, R. 1987. *Divorced Families.* New York: Norton.

Aldous, J. 1974. "The Making of Family Roles and Family Change." *Family Coordinator* 23:231–235.

———. 1985. "Parent–Adult Child Relations as Affected by Grandparenthood Status." In *Grandparenthood.* See Bengtson and Robertson 1985.

Anspach, D. 1976. "Kinship and Divorce." *Journal of Marriage and the Family* 38:343–350.

Apple, D. 1956. "The Social Structure of Grandparenthood." *American Anthropologist* 58:656–663.

Arling, G. 1976. "The Elderly Widow and Her Family and Friends." *Journal of Marriage and the Family* 38:757–768.

Bane, M. 1976. *Here to Stay: American Families in the Twentieth Century.* New York: Basic Books.

Barber, B. 1986. "United States of Anomie." *New Republic,* May 20, 33–35.

Bellah, R., Madsen, R., Sullivan, W., Swidler, A., and Tipton, S. 1985. *Habits of the Heart.* Berkeley and Los Angeles University of California Press.

Bender, D. 1967. "A Refinement of the Concept of Household, Families, Co-Residence, and Domestic Functions." *American Anthropologist* 69:494–504.

Bengtson, V. 1985. "The Diversity and Symbolism in Grandparents' Roles." In *Grandparenthood. See* Bengtson and Robertson 1985.

Bengtson, V., and Robertson, J., eds. 1985. *Grandparenthood: Emergent Perspectives on Traditional Roles.* Beverly Hills: Sage.

Berger, P., and Kellner, H. 1964. "Marriage and the Construction of Reality." *Diogenes* 46:1–25.

Blau, Z. 1973. *Old Age in a Changing Society.* New York: New Viewpoints.

Bohannon, P. 1971. *Divorce and After: An Analysis of the Emotional and Social Problems of Divorce.* New York: Anchor Books.

Boszormenyi-Nagy, I., and Spark, G. 1973. *Invisible Loyalties.* New York: Harper and Row.

Caplow, T., Bahr, H., Chadwick, B., Hill, R., and Williamson, M. 1982. *Middletown Families: Fifty Years of Change and Continuity.* Minneapolis: University of Minnesota Press.

Cherlin, A. 1978. "Remarriage as an Incomplete Institution." *American Journal of Sociology* 84:634–650.

———. 1983. "Family Policy: A Conservative Challenge and the Progressive Reform." *Journal of Family Issues* 4:427–438.

Cherlin, A., and Furstenberg, F. 1986. *American Grandparenthood.* New York: Basic Books.

Cicirelli, V. 1983a. "Adult Children and Their Elderly Parents." In *Family Relationships in Later Life,* ed. T. Brubaker. Beverly Hills: Sage.

———. 1983b. "A Comparison of Helping Behavior to Elderly Parents of Adult Children with Intact and Disrupted Marriages." *Gerontologist* 23:619–625.

Clark, M. 1969. "Cultural Values and Dependency in Later Life." In *The Dependencies of Older People,* ed. R. Kalish. Occasional Papers in Gerontology, no. 6. Ann Arbor, Michigan: Institute of Gerontology, University of Michigan.

Clark, M., and Anderson, B. 1967. *Culture and Aging.* Springfield, Ill.: Charles C. Thomas.

Cohen, R. 1971. *Dominance and Defiance: A Study of Marital Instability in an Islamic African Society.* Washington, D.C.: American Anthropological Association.

Cohen, S., and Syme, S., eds. 1985. *Social Support and Health.* New York: Academic Press.

Cohler, B. 1983. "Autonomy and Interdependence in the Family in Adulthood." *Gerontologist* 23:40–49.

Cohler, B., and Grunebaum, H. 1981. *Mothers, Grandmothers and Daughters.* New York: John Wiley.

Coser, R. 1974. "Authority and Structural Ambivalence in the Middle-Class Family." In *The Family: Its Structure and Functions,* ed. R. Coser. New York: St. Martin.

Cuber, J., and Haroff, P. 1965. *The Significant Americans* New York: Appleton-Century.

Dodson, F. 1981. *How to Grandparent.* New York: New American Library.

Dowd, J. 1980. "Exchange Rates and Older People." *Journal of Gerontology* 35:596–602.

Emerson, R. 1962. "Power and Dependency." *American Sociological Review* 27:31–40.

———. 1976. "Social Exchange Theory." In *Annual Review in Sociology,* ed. A. Inkeles and J. Coleman, vol. 2. Palo Alto, Calif.: Annual Reviews.

Farber, B. 1975. "Bilateral Kinship: Centripetal and Centrifugal Types of Organization." *Journal of Marriage and the Family* 39:227–242.

———. 1977. "Social Context, Kinship Mapping and Family Norms." *Journal of Marriage and the Family* 39:227–242.

———. 1981. *Conceptions of Kinship.* New York: Elsevier.

Fischer, C. 1982. *To Dwell among Friends.* Chicago: University of Chicago Press.

Fisher, L. 1981. "Transitions in the Mother-Daughter Relationship." *Journal of Marriage and the Family* 43:613–622.

Furstenberg, F. 1981. "Remarriage and Intergenerational Relations." In *Aging: Stability and Change in the Family,* ed. R. Fogel, E. Hatfield, S. Keesler, and E. Shanas. New York: Academic Press.

Furstenberg, F., and Spanier, G. 1984. *Recycling the Family: Remarriage after Divorce.* Beverly Hills: Sage.

Gans, H. 1974. *Popular Culture and High Culture: An Analysis and Evaluation of Taste.* New York: Basic Books.

Geertz, C. 1973. *The Interpretation of Culture.* New York: Free Press.

Gellner, E. 1957. "Ideal Language and Kinship Structures." *Philosophy of Science* 24:236–251.

————. 1960. "The Concept of Kinship." *Philosophy of Science* 27:187–204.

Glenn, N., and Supanic, M. 1984. "Social and Demographic Correlates of Divorce and Separation in the United States: An Update and Reconsideration." *Journal of Marriage and the Family* 46:563–576.

Glick, P., and Lin, S. 1986. "Recent Trends in Divorce and Remarriage." *Journal of Marriage and the Family* 48:737–748.

Gluckman, M. 1951. "Kinship and Marriage among the Lozi of Northern Rhodesia and the Zulu of Nale." In *African Kinship Systems of Kinship and Marriage*, ed. A. Radcliffe-Brown. London: Oxford University Press.

Goode, W. 1956. *Women in Divorce*. New York: Free Press.

————. 1959. "Theoretical Importance of Love." *American Sociological Review* 24:38–47.

Gouldner, A. 1960. "The Norm of Reciprocity: A Preliminary Statement." *American Sociological Review* 25:161–178.

Hagestad, G. 1981. "Problems and Promises in the Social Psychology of Intergenerational Relations." In *Aging: Stability and Change in the Family*, ed. R. Fogel, E. Hatfield, S. Keesler, and E. Shanas. New York: Academic Press.

Hess, B., and Waring, J. 1978. "Parent and Child in Later Life: Rethinking the Relationship." In *Child Influences on Marital and Family Interaction*, ed. R. Lerner and G. Spanier. New York: Academic Press.

Hess, R., and Handel, G. 1967. "The Family as a Psychosocial Organization." In *The Psychological Interior of the Family*, ed. R. Hess and G. Handel, 10–24. Chicago: Aldine.

Hetherington, M., Cox, E., and Cox, R. 1982. "Effects of Divorce on Parents and Children." In *Nontraditional Families*, ed. M. Lamb. Hillsdale, N.J.: Lawrence Erlbaum.

Hicks, M., and Platt, M. 1971. "Marital Happiness and Stability: A Review." In *A Decade of Family Research and Action*, ed. C. Broderick. Minneapolis: National Council of Family Relations.

Johnson, C. 1974. "Alternatives to Alienation: A Japanese-American Example." In *Alienation: Context, Term, and Meaning*, ed. F. Johnson. New York: Seminar Press.

————. 1978. "Interdependence, Reciprocity, and Indebtedness: An Analysis of Japanese-American Kinship Relations." *Journal of Marriage and the Family* 39:351–363.

————. 1983a. "A Cultural Analysis of the Grandmother." *Research on Aging* 5:547–567.

————. 1983b. "Dyadic Family Relations and Social Supports." *Gerontologist* 23:377–383.

————. 1985a. "Grandparenting Options in Divorcing Families." In *Grandparenthood*. See Bengtson and Robertson 1985.

————. 1985b. *Growing Up and Growing Old in Italian-American Families*. New Brunswick, N.J.: Rutgers University Press.

————. 1988a. "Active and Latent Functions of Grandparenting during the Divorce Process." *Gerontologist* 28:185–191.

————. 1988b. "Definitions of Family and Kinship with Divorce and Remarriage." In *The Semiotic-Bridge: Trends from California,* ed. I. Rauch and G. Carr. Berlin: Mouton de Guyter. In press.

————. 1988c. "Post-Divorce Reorganization of the Relationships between the Divorced and Their Parents." *Journal of Marriage and the Family* 50:221–231.

————. 1988d. "Socially Controlled Civility: Intergenerational Relations during the Divorce Process." *American Behavioral Sciences*. In press.

Johnson, C., and Barer, B. 1987. "American Kinship Relationships with Divorce and Remarriage." *Gerontologist* 27:330–335.

Johnson, C., and Catalano, D. 1983. "A Longitudinal Study of Family Supports." *Gerontologist* 23:612–618.

Johnson, C., Schmidt, C., and Klee, L. 1988. "Conceptions of Parentage and Kinship among Children of Divorce." *American Anthropologist* 90:24–32.

Kahana, E., and Kahana, B. 1970. "Grandparenthood from the Perspective of the Developing Grandchild." *Journal of Aging and Human Development* 2:261–268.

Kahana, R., and Levin, S. 1971. "Aging and the Conflict of Generations." *Journal of Geriatric Psychiatry* 4:115–135.

Kivett, V. 1985. "Consanguinity and Kin Level: Their Relative Importance to Helping Networks of Old Adults." *Journal of Gerontology* 40:228–234.

Kivnick, H. 1982. "Grandparenthood: Meaning and Mental Health." *Gerontologist* 22:59–66.

Kornhaber, A., and Woodward, K. 1981. *Grandparents/Grandchildren: The Vital Connection*. Garden City, N.J.: Anchor Books.

La Gaipa, J. 1981. "A Systems Approach to Personal Relationships." In

Personal Relationships. Vol. 1, *Studying Personal Relationships,* ed. S. Duck and R. Gilmour. New York: Academic Press.

Lasch, C. 1978. *The Culture of Narcissism.* New York: Norton.

———. 1979. *Haven in a Heartless World: The Family Besieged.* New York: Basic Books.

———. 1984. *The Minimal Self: Psychic Survival in Troubled Times.* New York: Norton.

Laslett, B. 1978. "Family Membership, Past and Present." *Social Problems* 25:476–490.

Lenz, E. 1987. "The Generation Gap from Persephone to Portnoy." *New York Times,* October 30.

Levinger, G. 1965. "Marital Cohesiveness and Dissolution: An Integrative Review." *Journal of Marriage and the Family* 27:19–28.

———. 1979. "A Social Psychological Perspective on Marital Dissolution." In *Divorce and Separation,* ed. G. Levinger and O. Moles. New York: Basic Books.

Longfellow, C. 1979. "Divorce in Context: Its Impact on Children." In *Divorce and Separation,* ed. G. Levinger and O. Moles. New York: Basic Books.

Lowenthal, M., and Haven, C. 1968. "Interaction and Adaptation: Intimacy as a Critical Variable." *American Sociological Review* 33:20–30.

Macklin, E. 1983. "Nonmarital Heterosexual Cohabitation: An Overview." In *Contemporary Families and Alternate Life Styles,* ed. E. Macklin and R. Rubin. Beverly Hills: Sage.

McLanahan, B., Wedemeyer, N., and Adelberg, T. 1981. "Network Structure, Social Support, and Psychological Well-Being in the Single-Parent Family." *Journal of Marriage and the Family* 43:601–612.

Merton, R., and Barbar, E. 1963. "Sociological Ambivalence." In *Sociological Theory: Values and Sociocultural Change,* ed. E. Tiryakian. New York: Free Press.

Murdock, G. 1949. *Social Structure.* New York: MacMillan.

Neugarten, B., and Weinstein, M. 1964. "The Changing American Grandparent." *Journal of Marriage and the Family* 26:199–204.

Newcomb, M., and Bentler, P. 1981. "Marital Breakdown." In *Personal Relationships.* Vol. 3, *Personal Relationships in Disorder,* ed. S. Duck and R. Gilmour. New York: Academic Press.

Norton, A., and Moorman, J. 1987. "Current Trends in Marriage and Divorce among American Women." *Journal of Marriage and the Family* 49:3–14.

Paine, R. 1974. "An Exploratory Analysis of Middle-class Friendship."
In *The Compact,* ed. E. Leyton. Newfoundland Social and Economic
Papers no. 3. Memorial University of Newfoundland.

Parsons, T. 1949. "The Social Structure of the Family." In *The Family:
Its Function and Destiny,* ed. R. Anshen. New York: Harper and Row.

Quinton, A. 1983. "Culture and Character." *New Republic,* October 17,
26–29.

Radcliff-Brown, A. 1952. *Structure and Function in Primitive Society.* New
York: Free Press.

Riesman, D., Glazer, N., and Denney, R. 1950. *The Lonely Crowd.*
New Haven, Conn.: Yale University Press.

Robertson, J. 1977. "Grandmotherhood: A Study of Role Conceptions."
Journal of Marriage and the Family 39:165–174.

Rosenmayr, L. 1972. "The Elderly in Austrian Society." In *Aging and
Modernization,* ed. D. Cowgill and L. Holmes. New York: Appleton-
Century and Crofts.

Rossi, A. 1977. "A Biosocial Perspective on Parenting." *Daedalus*
106:1–31.

Schneider, D. 1965. "American Kinship Terms for Kinsmen: A Critique
of Goodnough's Componential Analysis of Yankee Kinship Terminology." *American Anthropologist* 67:288–318.

———. 1968. *American Kinship: A Cultural Account.* Englewood Cliffs,
N.J.: Prentice-Hall.

Schneider, D., and Cottrell, C. 1975. *The American Kin Universe: A
Genealogical Study.* Chicago: Department of Anthropology, University
of Chicago.

Schneider, D., and Homans, G. 1955. "Kinship Terminology and the
American Kinship System." *American Anthropologist* 57:1194–1208.

Seeley, J., Sim, R., and Loosley, E. 1956. *Crestwood Heights.* New York:
Basic Books.

Shanas, E. 1979. "Social Myth as Hypothesis: The Case of the Family
Relations of Older People." *Gerontologist* 19:3–9.

Slater, P. 1970. *Pursuit of Loneliness.* Boston: Beacon Press.

———. 1974. "Parental Role Differentiation." In *The Family: Its Structure and Functions,* ed. R. Coser. New York: St. Martin.

Spicer, J., and Hampe, G. 1975. "Kinship Interaction after Divorce."
Journal of Marriage and the Family 37:113–119.

Sprey, J., and Matthews, S. 1982. "Contemporary Grandparenthood: A
Systemic Transition." *Middle and Late Life Transitions.* ed. F. Berardo.

Annals of the American Academy of Political and Social Science 464:91–103.

Sussman, M. 1968. "Relationships of Adult Children with Their Parents in the United States." In *Social Structure and the Family: Generational Relations*, ed. E. Shanas and G. Streib. Englewood Cliffs, N.J.: Prentice-Hall.

———. 1985. "The Family Life of Older People." In *Handbook of Aging and the Social Sciences*, ed. R. Binstock and E. Shanas. New York: Van Nostrand Reinhold.

Sussman, M., and Burchinal, L. 1962. "Kin Family Network: Unheralded Conceptualization of Family Functioning." *Marriage and Family Living* 24:231–240.

Sweetser, D. 1964. "Asymmetry in Intergenerational Family Relationships." *Social Forces* 43:346–352.

Swidler, A. 1986. "Culture in Action: Symbols and Strategies." *American Sociological Review* 51:273–286.

Taubin, S., and Mudd, E. 1983. "Contemporary Traditional Families: The Undefined Majority." In *Contemporary Families and Alternate Life Styles*, ed. E. Macklin and R. Rubin. Beverly Hills: Sage.

Troll, L. 1980a. "Grandparenting." In *Aging in the 1980s*, ed. L. Poon. Washington, D.C.: American Psychological Association.

———. 1980b. "Intergenerational Relations in Later Life: A Family Systems Approach." In *Transitions in Aging*, ed. N. Datan and N. Lohmann. New York: Academic Press.

———. 1982. "Family Life in Middle and Old Age: The Generation Gap." *Middle and Late Life Transitions*, ed. F. Berardo. *Annals of the American Academy of Political and Social Sciences* 464:1–187.

Troll, L., and Bengtson, V. 1979. "Generations in Families." In *Contemporary Theories about the Family*, ed. W. Burr, R. Hill, F. Nye, and I. Reiss. New York: Free Press.

Troll, L., Miller, S., and Atchley, R. 1979. *Families in Later Life*. Belmont, Calif.: Wadsworth, 1979.

Troll, L., and Smith, J. 1976. "Attachment through the Life Span: Some Questions about Dyadic Bonds among Adults." *Human Development* 19:156–170.

Turner, R. 1970. *Family Interaction*. New York: Wiley.

———. 1976. "The Real Self: From Institution to Impulse." *American Journal of Sociology* 81:989–1016.

van der Veen, C. 1971. "Ambivalence, Social Structure, and Dominant

Kinship Relationships." In *Kinship and Culture,* ed. F. Hsu. Chicago: Aldine, 1971.

Verbrugge, L. 1979. "Marital Status and Health." *Journal of Marriage and the Family* 41:267–285.

Walker, K., and Messinger, L. 1979. "Remarriage after Divorce: Dissolution and Reconstruction of Family Boundaries." *Family Process* 18:186–192.

Wallerstein, J. 1984. "Children of Divorce: Preliminary Report of a Ten-Year Follow-Up of Young Children." *American Journal of Orthopsychiatry* 54:444–458.

Wallerstein, J., and Corbin, S. 1986. "Father-Child Relationships after Divorce: Child Support and Educational Opportunity." *Family Law Quarterly* 22:109–128.

Wallerstein, J., and Kelly, J. 1979. "Children of Divorce: A Review." *Social Work* 24:468–475.

Weed, J. 1979. "Implications of Divorce and Remarriage for Physical Health of the Aged and Their Adult Children." Presentation of the Gerontological Society of America, Washington, D.C.

Weigert, A., and Hastings, R. 1977. "Identity Loss, Family, and Social Change." *American Journal of Sociology* 82:1171–1185.

Weiss, R. 1979. "The Emotional Impact of Marital Separation." In *Divorce and Separation,* ed. G. Levinger and O. Moles. New York: Basic Books.

Weitzman, L. 1985. *The Divorce Revolution: The Unexpected Social and Economic Consequences for Women and Children in America.* New York: Free Press.

Weitzman, L., and Dixon, R. 1980. "The Transformation of Legal Marriage through No-Fault Divorce." In *The Family in Transition,* ed. A. Skolnick and J. Skolnick. Boston: Little, Brown.

Wilson, K., and Deshane, M. 1982. "The Legal Rights of Grandparents: A Preliminary Discussion." *Gerontologist* 22 (1) 67–71.

Wood, V., and Robertson, J. 1978. "Friendship and Kinship Interaction: Differential Effect on the Morale of the Elderly." *Journal of Marriage and the Family* 40:367–375.

Wordick, F. 1973. "Another View of American Kinship." *American Anthropologist* 75:1634–1657.

Wylie, P. 1979. *Generation of Vipers.* New York: Larem Press.

Yanigasako, S. 1977. "Women-centered Kin Networks in Urban Bilateral Kinship Systems." *American Ethnologist* 4:207–226.

INDEX

Adams, R., 9, 12
affinal relatives (relationship by marriage). *See* in-laws
age: image of grandparents and, 99–101; study sample and, 25
Ahrons, C., 63, 65, 180
Aldous, J., 5, 98
Anspach, D., 89
Apple, D., 88
assets, division of, 65
Atchlev, R., 167
authority (decline of), 7–8
autonomy, 44

babysitting, 130, 147, 150
Bane, M., 2
Barber, B., 7, 122, 139
Barer, B., 13, 58, 89, 105, 171, 174, 181
belief systems, divorce and, 68–69
Bellah, R., 2, 7, 8
Bender, D., 10
Bengston, V., 14, 87, 116, 126
Bentler, P., 65
Berger, P., 121
Blau, Z., 88, 138
Bohannon, P., 12, 168
Boszormenyi-Nagy, I., 117

Bowman, M., 180
Burchinal, L., 167

Caplow, T., 1, 2
Catalano, D., 194
Cherlin, A., 22, 63, 88, 110, 187
child-parent relationship. *See* intergenerational relationships
childrearing practices, 185, 191; grandparents and, 135
children: custody of minor, 66, 85; divorce process and, 65, 73, 77, 78, 85–86; economic dependence on parents and, 129; family structure and, 10–12, 13; family unit and, 3, 13; number of (study sample), 25; parents and married, 3–4; stepchildren, 27
children (grandchildren): abandoned (example of), 151; advice from grandparents about, 158; grandfather and, 109–110; grandparenting styles and, 89–91, 92, 99; grandparent response to divorce and, 103, 189, 190; intergenerational involvement

children (*cont.*)
and, 105–108; remarriage
and, 173, 175, 178–179
child support, 65
Cicirelli, V., 116
Clark, M., 139
Cohen, R., 62, 167
Cohen, S., 133
Cohler, B., 117
Corbin, S., 62, 65
Coser, R., 139
Cottrell, C., 10, 169
Cox, E., 20, 62
Cox, R., 20, 62
Cuber, J., 69
cultural content of family relationships: data collection and
research and, 7; defining culture and, 6; family structure
and, 184, 186; independence
and dependence and, 8; new
American character type and,
7–8
cultural directives: divorce and
changing, 33–39; genera-
tional differences and, 45–48;
grandparents and life-style of
their children and, 42–45;
research and, 28

data analysis, 30–31
data collection, 7
dating, 74. *See also* romantic relationships
daughter-in-law, mother-in-
law's coalition with, 175–
176, 182. *See also* in-laws
daughters: depression and, 133;
economic aid and, 122,

125–126, 127, 128–131,
134–135; intergenerational
relationships and, 121–122,
128–130, 135–137; mothers
as friends of, 51, 53, 193;
redefining relationship with
parent and, 142, 143–146,
147–148, 150–152, 156–
157
decision making (divorce process), 66
demographic changes (family
structure), 1–2
Denney, R., 7
dependency, 188, 190, 193;
cultural content of family relationships and, 8; intergenerational relationships and,
119, 128–130, 141, 146,
147, 149–152, 153, 158
Deshane, M., 87
destiny, 34–35
developmental cycle, 2
divorce process: common types
of divorce and, 75–76;
conflictual (acrimonious) case
history of, 79–80; dating
and romantic relationships
and, 74; decision-making criteria and, 66; efforts to save
marriages and, 70–72;
finding causes of divorce and,
67–70; historical background
on, 62; legal definition of
family and, 65; legal definition of marriage and, 64; limit
on sanctions against, 72–73;
long-term deliberation case
history of, 76–78; marital

changes and, 62; marital conflict resolution and, 66–67; research and, 62; social guidelines and, 63; social pressure and, 67; stages in, 65–66; unintentional breakdown case history of, 80–84, 188
Dixon, R., 64
dyadic relationships, family structure and, 5, 29

economic aid: children's dependence on parents and, 122, 125–126, 127, 128–131, 134–135; dependence and, 150–152; grandparents and, 95, 111; to parent, 119, 126–127; remarriage and, 53–54
economic problems, 41, 56–57
education (study sample), 25, 72
elderly, 2
Emerson, R., 129, 130
emotional support. See support
employment. See work
Erhard Seminar Training (est), 37, 42
ethnicity, 21

family role models, grandparents as, 101–102
family roles (kinship system reorganization), 179–182
family structure: cultural content of family relationships and, 6–9; defining, 65; demographic changes and, 1–2; divorce and changes in, 5, 9–14; dyadic relationships

and, 5, 29; family reorganization and, 15–17; family unit analysis and, 9–14; grandparents and divorce and, 14; inconsistent views on, 4–5; marital instability and, 12; as nuclear unit, 2–4, 9, 10, 13; study conclusions and, 185–187
family structure reorganization: boundary changes and, 15–17, 188, 192; generational bond and, 15, 49–54; loose-knit networks and, 56–60; nuclear family and, 15, 54–56; research and, 23–24; stability or change in relationships and, 48–49; value systems and, 60–61
Farber, B., 49
fathers; economic aid and, 126; as grandparents, 109–110
finances (divorce process analysis), 65, 73, 84–85
financial aid. See economic aid
financial problems, 41, 56–57
Fischer, C., 120
friends: divorce and, 36–37, 85; mothers as, 51, 53, 193; support and, 49
Furstenberg, F., 13, 22, 63, 88, 108, 110, 166, 167, 168, 172

Gans, H., 8
Geertz, C., 5, 6, 32
Gellner, E., 9
gift giving, 144–145
Glazer, N., 7

Glenn, N., 68, 73
Glick, P., 62
Gluckman, M., 167
Goode, William, 63, 68, 69
good life concept, 33–34
Gouldner, A., 8
grandparents: abandoned grandchild example and, 151;
  advice from, 158; autonomy
  and, 44; concept of self and,
  45–48; divorce and, 14;
  divorced, 73; expansion of
  kinship system and, 169,
  180–181; extramarital affairs
  of children and, 76; as family
  role models, 101–102;
  grandfathers and, 109–110;
  grandmother and intergenerational relationships and, 98,
  105–108; grandmother as
  "kin-keeper" and, 174; grandmother's role and attitude
  changes and, 103–105, 111,
  112; grandparenting expectations vs. realities and, 110–
  113, 114; grandparenting
  norms and, 95, 96, 97–98;
  grandparenting styles and,
  89–92; identifying causes of
  divorce and, 93–95; image of
  (age norms), 99–101; as
  norm-directed role, 95–99;
  privacy and, 44; redefining
  role of (after divorce of
  children), 103–110; religion
  and, 43; research (study) and,
  20–21, 24, 27, 28, 29; response to divorce of children

of, 92–93, 102–103; role
  confusion and, 112–113,
  114–115; satisfaction with
  role of, 108–109; study conclusions and, 187–188,
  189–190; value systems and,
  42, 45. See also children
  (grandchildren); intergenerational relationships
Grunebaum, H., 117

Habits of the Heart (Bellah), 2
Hagestad, G., 116, 153
Hampe, G., 88
Handel, G., 5
Haroff, P., 69
Hastings, R., 4
Haven, C., 133
Here to Stay (Bane), 2
Hess, B., 5, 116
Hetherington, M., 20, 62
Homans, G., 166
How to Grandparent (Dodson),
  87

impulse-directed individuals,
  186
independence, 183; cultural
  content of family relationships and, 8; intergenerational relationships and, 122,
  130, 131, 132, 134, 146,
  159; study conclusions and,
  187–188
in-laws: bounded nucleated unit
  and, 55; coalition with
  daughter-in-law and, 175–
  176, 182; divorce and family

structure and, 13, 14; grandparents and, 89, 93, 133, 136; loose-knit networks and, 57, 58; research and, 25, 29. *See also* kinship system reorganization

intergenerational relationships, 5, 14; ambivalent relations example of, 161–162; comparing child and parent and, 121–122; concept of self and, 47; conflict analysis and, 146–149, 191, 194; conflictual relations example of, 153, 155–156, 160, 161; dependence and, 119, 128–130, 141, 146, 147, 149–152, 153, 158; economic aid to child and, 122, 125–126, 127, 128–131, 134–135; economic aid to parent and, 119, 126–127; emotional support and, 133–134, 134–135; family structure reorganization and, 15, 49–54; friendly relations example of, 153, 154–155; general analysis (background on) and, 118–121; incongruent expectations and, 131, 132–133; independence and, 122, 130, 131, 132, 134, 146, 159; mother and child gender difference and, 135; noninterference and, 132, 137; power relationships and, 128–131; privacy of nuclear family and, 123–124, 127, 128; rene-

gotiation of relationships and, 131, 141–146; research and, 29; sexual relationships (views on) and, 47, 48, 52; social contact and, 124, 127–128; study conclusions and, 184–185, 190–192; tension (control of) and, 192–195; value systems and, 42–48, 52. *See also* grandparents; kinship system reorganization

interview (study), 24–25, 27–30

Johnson, C., 8, 9, 13, 49, 58, 65, 89, 95, 103, 105, 107, 111, 120, 171, 174, 179, 181, 194

Journal of Marriage and the Family, 62, 186

Kahana, B., 88
Kahana, E., 88
Kahana, R., 117
Karma, 34–35
Kellner, H., 121
Kelly, J., 12, 20, 62
kinship system: family structure and divorce and, 9–14; grandmother as "kin-keeper" and, 174; grandparents and expansion of, 169, 180–181; loose-knit network and, 166–168; nuclear family and, 166–168

kinship system reorganization, 189, 191; contraction with divorce and, 171–172;

kinship reorganization (*cont.*)
divorcing parents in expanding system and, 181–182; expansion by coalition with in-laws and, 174–176; expansion by divorce and remarriage and, 173–174; expansion by divorce and remarriage of multiple siblings and, 176–178; family roles and, 179–182; grandparents and divorce and, 105–108; grandparents in expanding system and, 180–181; kinship system expansion and, 169; models of, 169–171; relatives of divorce and remarriage and, 168–169, 170, 171; replacement with remarriage and, 172–173; two-generation divorce and remarriage chains and, 178–179
Kivett, V., 110
Kivnick, H., 88
Klee, L., 65, 179
Kornhaber, A., 87

La Gaipa, J., 14, 139
Lasch, C., 7, 8
Laslett, B., 2, 4
Lenz, E., 185
Levinger, G., 63, 65, 66
Levin, S., 117
life-styles, 72, 193; causes of divorce and, 94; grandparents and cultural directives and, 42–45; research sample and, 21

Lin, S., 62
Longfellow, C., 12, 62
loose-knit network of relationships, 16; family reorganization and, 56–60; intergenerational relationships and, 128; kinship system and, 166–168; remarriage and, 57; sex and, 58, 59; value systems and, 58–59
Lowenthal, M., 133

Macklin, E., 2
marital instability, family structure and, 12
marriage: antifamilism and profamilism and, 2–3; defining, 64; efforts to save, 70–72; parent's approval of, 93; self-fulfillment and, 187
Matthews, S., 88, 89
Merton, R., 122, 139
Messinger, L., 5
Miller, S., 167
mothers (of divorced individuals): depression of daughters and, 133; economic aid and, 119, 126–127; as friends, 51, 53, 193; intergenerational relations and, 121–122, 128–130, 135–137; redefining relationship with daughters and, 142, 143–146, 147–148, 150–152, 156–157; redefining relationship with sons and, 148–149, 152, 154–156, 157, 158–160
Mudd, E., 1
Murdock, G., 9

Neugarten, B., 88, 96, 110
Newcomb, M., 65
no-fault divorce, 64, 65, 69
noninterference, 183; intergenerational relationships and,
  132, 137; study conclusions
  and, 188, 194
nuclear family: family reorganization and, 15, 54–56;
  family structure and, 2–4,
  9, 10, 13; kinship system
  and, 166–168; privacy of,
  16, 92, 95, 123–124, 127,
  128, 153

Paine, R., 14
parent-child relationship. See intergenerational relationships
Parsons, T., 3
personal growth, 38
power relationships, 128, 131
privacy, 44
privacy of nuclear family. See
  nuclear family, privacy of
projective story technique,
  45–47
psychological guidelines, 34

Quinton, A., 7

Radcliffe-Brown, A., 166
religion: grandparents and, 43;
  study sample and, 25
remarriage, 128, 151, 184, 187;
  children and, 173, 175, 178–
  179; complications in, 159–
  160; divorce process analysis
  and, 63, 70; financial assistance and, 53–54; kinship

reorganization and, 168–169,
  170, 171, 172–173, 173–
  174, 176–178, 192; loose-
  knit networks and, 57; research and, 27
remarriage chains, 158, 193;
  kinship reorganization and,
  178–179
research: cultural content of
  family relationships and, 7;
  cultural directives and, 28;
  data analysis and, 30–31;
  divorce process and, 62; interview and, 24–25, 27–30;
  projective story technique
  and, 45–47; sample characteristics and, 25–27; sample
  selection and, 22–25; sample
  size and, 21; techniques used
  in design of, 19–22
Riesman, D., 7, 186
Robertson, J., 14, 88, 110, 138
Rodgers, R., 63
romantic relationships, 36–37,
  38–39, 74
Rosenmayr, L., 3–4
Rossi, A., 187

sample (study), selection, size,
  and characteristics of, 21–27
Schmidt, C., 65, 179
Schneider, D., 5, 10, 166, 168,
  169
Seeley, J., 3
self: divorce and change in concept of, 34, 35; generational
  differences and, 47; grandparents and concept of, 45–48
settlement, 65

sexual relations: changing concept of, 35–36; extramarital, 76; generational differences and, 47, 48, 52; loose-knit networks and, 58, 59; parents' (of divorced individuals) awareness of problems with, 93; problems with (as cause of divorce), 70, 77
Shanas, E., 12
Slater, P., 7, 185
social activities, 52, 53, 85
social change and divorce, 184
social contact (intergenerational), 124, 127–128
social guidelines (divorce process), 63
social pressure, 67
social support. *See* support (social and emotional)
socioeconomic status (of study sample), 21, 22, 25, 68
sons: mothers and, 121, 123, 128–130, 135, 136; redefining relationship with parent and, 148–149, 152, 154–156, 157, 158–160
Spanier, G., 63, 172
Sparks, G., 117
Spicer, J., 88
Spock, B., 185
Sprey, J., 88, 89
stepchildren, 27. *See also* children
stress (after divorce), 85
study sample, selection, size, and characteristics of, 21–27
Supanic, M., 68, 73
support (social and emotional),

20, 194; changing values and, 36–37, 38; divorce process and, 85; family reorganization and, 49; intergenerational tensions and 133–134, gender differences and 134–135, 144. *See also* economic aid
Sussman, M., 4, 10, 120, 167
Sweetser, D., 174
Swidler, A., 6
Syme, S., 133

Taubin, S., 1
tension, control of intergenerational, 192–195
therapy, 37, 40; range of techniques of, 70–71
Troll, L., 87, 97, 116, 126, 167
Turner, R., 4, 7, 186

Values, 193; causes of divorce and, 68; changing (of divorced individuals), 33–39; divorce histories (attitudinal changes) and, 39–42; family reorganization and, 60–61; generational differences and, 45–48; grandparents and, 42–45; loose-knit networks and, 58–59

Walker, K., 5
Wallerstein, J., 12, 20, 62, 65
Waring, J., 116
Weed, J., 12, 20, 168
Weigert, A., 4
Weinstein, M., 88, 96, 110

Weiss, R., 67

Weitzman, L., 64, 65

Wilson, K., 87

women's roles, 2

Wood, V., 88, 138

Woodward, K., 87

Wordick, F., 167

work: sample characteristics and, 25–26; women and, 2

Wylie, P., 116

Yanigasako, S., 167, 183